Praise for *In the Eye of the Storm*

"Gene Robinson is the most controversial Christian in the world, yet if you did not know one thing about him — his sexuality — you would think him no different from thousands of other ministers, priests, pastors, or indeed bishops and archbishops. And he's not — merely more open and candid than they dare to be. Whether you agree with Bishop Robinson or not, his beliefs are important for all to know. In this book he shows there is much more about him and his faith than the single issue of sexual orientation."

> — **Stephen Bates,** religious affairs correspondent for the *Guardian* newspaper, London, 2000–2007, and British religious writer of the year in 2005 and 2006

"Gene Robinson is no revolutionary: he upholds marriage as a sacred covenant, but knows the same covenant theology can include same-sex partnerships too. For living this truth he has been scapegoated — not for being the first gay bishop, but the first honest one. By God's grace he has stayed strong, still trying to love his enemies into friends. One day the Church will understand what it owes him."

> — **The Very Rev. Jeffrey John,** Dean, St. Alban's Cathedral, England

"This book's dramatic expression of Gene's commitment to gay and lesbian inclusion within the Church is central to its theme. While acknowledging the pain and loneliness of this struggle, he gives thanks that in the Incarnation and Resurrection God's will is being made known to the reconciliation of a broken Anglican Communion."

> — **Edmond Browning,** 24th Presiding Bishop, Episcopal Church USA

"Those who vilify and those who glorify Bishop Gene Robinson solely because of his sexuality need to read this book. Bishop Robinson's powerful witness to God's mission of reconciliation in Jesus Christ through the power of the Holy Spirit challenges us all to go beyond the confines of single identity politics by seeing ourselves as both oppressor and oppressed, enslaved and free, sinful and forgiven."

> — **The Rev. Ian T. Douglas,** Ph.D., Angus Dun Professor of Mission and World Christianity, Episcopal Divinity School, Cambridge, Massachusetts

"This book is part of a new reality: Gene Robinson has become a recognizable global icon. Here is his testament of truth. He speaks from the heart about many issues and emerges as honest, highly readable, down-to-earth, and courageous. Clearly he's also a symbolic person, perhaps already an archetype. I am deeply grateful for his vulnerability and authenticity."

> — **Malcolm Boyd,** writer-in-residence at the Cathedral Center of St. Paul, Los Angeles, and author of the spiritual classic *Are You Running with Me, Jesus?*

"In this spirited, spiritual, and life-affirming book, Bishop Robinson writes movingly about his faith, his journey, and the challenges and blessings of being an openly gay bishop committed to his Church and to social justice."
— **Kevin M. Cathcart,** Executive Director, Lambda Legal

"As Joshua stood before the Israelites at the edge of Canaan, again and again he told them, 'Be strong and courageous.' With heart-wrenching stories and compelling biblical insight, Gene Robinson has issued another such clarion call, demanding a courageous faith and asking us to choose whether we will serve a God of love or a God of fear. The Promised Land of Christian unity depends on our answer." — **Rev. Anne Robertson,** Executive Director of the Massachusetts Bible Society and author of *Blowing the Lid Off the God-Box*

"This is Gene Robinson's own story, told with simplicity and humility and revealing his passionate faith. He recounts how his experience has made him particularly close to vulnerable groups, such as the inmates of a women's prison, and how we all need one another for our very salvation. This honest account will encourage anyone seriously committed to the message of Jesus, and shows him deeply committed within the Anglican Communion even to those who vilify him." — **Richard Harries,** former Bishop of Oxford and Professor of Theology, King's College, London

"Bishop Robinson takes the reader on a rare and inspirational journey into the heart and soul of a deeply spiritual being. In authentic and prosaic style, the book provides a prophetic vision of God's love for all humankind. The author's open vulnerability to and knowledge of the love of God is alive in these pages. I was touched and inspired by this book."
— **Bonnie Anderson,** president of the Episcopal House of Deputies

"Gene Robinson opens his soul to us and takes us inside one of the most compelling issues of our day. Gene Robinson's humility, honesty, and courage are evident on every page. This book will give biblical insight to many, end searches, and give light to those who sit in darkness."
— **Joan Brown Campbell,** former director of the U.S. office of the World Council of Churches, chair of the department of religion at the historic Chautauqua Institution and chair of the Global Women's Peace Initiative

"This book eloquently reaffirms the simple truth that God's love protects ALL OF US in the eye of any storm. It also chronicles how God's love continues to melt away prejudice, intolerance, and hatred in today's world."
— **Dick Gephardt,** former U.S. Representative from Missouri, House Majority Leader from 1995 to 2003

"An astonishing book, written straight from the eye of the cultural storm and, more importantly, straight from the heart of a man of great faith who finds his own church willing to fracture itself over the misguided exclusion of people who, like him, are gay. A clarion call to the Anglican Church and to all Christians to reconnect with the essence of their faith — the example of a radically inclusive love that embraces us all." — **Bradley Whitford,** actor, *The West Wing*

"A fast, facile read — but beneath Bishop Robinson's simple words lies a depth of un-probed truths that reveal real causes of the Anglican Communion's deep divisions, the difficult path to reconciliation and the challenge of our call to Christian discipleship in the global village."
— **Barbara C. Harris,** Bishop Suffragan Massachusetts (Ret.)

"In this wonderful and wise book, the message of Christianity becomes shockingly real and amazingly positive yet truly challenging. Bishop Robinson is so articulately simple because he so clearly embodies his own message."
— **Judith Light,** actress

"In his ebullient celebration of faith, Bishop Robinson makes a clarion call to action. By reminding us that we are all children of God, he urges a life of greater compassion and acceptance not only of lgbt people but of disenfranchised persons everywhere."
— **Joe Solmonese,** president of the Human Rights Campaign

"Long before Gene Robinson was an international icon, many of us had the good fortune of receiving fortification for our journeys by his so generously sharing with us his journey. Founded on the bedrock of durably infectious and joyful faith, a devotional relationship with scripture, healthy church leadership, prophetic peace and justice pioneering, Gene was an unofficial bishop to many before the Spirit ever whispered his name to the diocese of New Hampshire. In this book Gene has illuminatingly drawn the contours of his animating faith. Here he reveals the secrets of that unbelievably calm centeredness from which emanates his courage, tenacity, effervescence, and that holy love he expresses for all — even for his detractors. This is nothing short of sacred reading — *lectio divina.*" — **Rev. Ed Bacon,** Rector, Pasadena, California

"In this book, Bishop Robinson offers us an account of both his belief in and understanding of the gospel. It is honest, compelling, and accessible. We can see the wide-ranging perspective of his theology. His commitment to the redeeming love of God permeates every facet of his life: his family, the church, the outcast, and those who condemn him. He is truly a remarkable man. Here is the opportunity to know him in his own words."
— **The Right Rev. Jane Holmes Dixon,**
Senior Advisor for Inter Religious Affairs,
The Interfaith Alliance

"Those who know Gene Robinson will relish this book. Those who don't know him will find here a Christian overflowing with life, insight, commitment, and passion."   — Marcus Borg, best-selling author of many books, including *The Heart of Christianity*

"Gene Robinson's message of hope, justice, and reconciliation is broader than one topic, more powerful than one issue. Gene shows us how to be not just effective advocates for a cause, but good citizens of this world on our way to the next."
        — Harry Knox, Director, Religion and Faith Program, Human Rights Campaign Foundation

"Gene Robinson's *In the Eye of the Storm* is grounds for the conversation that most people want and most people need on the subject of what it means to be gay and Christian in both church and society. It is an honest rendering of personal experience and biblical and theological interpretations in tension with heterosexist society. It raises questions of sexuality and sexual orientation, of theology and morality, that every human being, whatever their sexual preference, needs to face if they are going to be both fully human and truly Christian. It is not a screed. This book is a gift to the entire Christian community. It enables a person to listen, to think, to be more honest with themselves and more gentle with others. And, if nothing else, *In the Eye of the Storm* is a must for those who really want to understand what's going on in churches today — and why."
        — Joan Chittister, O.S.B., international lecturer on contemporary spirituality and author of many books, including *WomanStrength: Modern Church, Modern Women*

"Many of those who express opinions about Gene Robinson don't know the first thing about him as a human being, a man of faith, or a bishop. Nor have they walked in his shoes. This book reveals the extraordinary grace of God at work in the life and witness of a courageous Christian."
        — Bishop Michael Ingham, Diocese of New Westminster, Canada

In the
EYE
of the
STORM
Swept to the Center by God

GENE ROBINSON

Foreword by
Archbishop Desmond Tutu

SEABURY BOOKS
New York

Unless otherwise noted, the scripture quotations contained herein are from the New Revised Standard Version Bible, copyright © 1989 by the Division of Christian Education of the National Council of Churches of Christ in the U.S.A. Used by permission. All rights reserved.

Cover photograph by Weiqin Bao
Cover design by Laurie Klein Westhafer
Interior design by John Eagleson

Seabury Books
An imprint of Church Publishing Incorporated
445 Fifth Avenue
New York, NY 10016
www.churchpublishing.org

Library of Congress Cataloging-in-Publication Data

Robinson, V. Gene, 1947-
    In the eye of the storm : swept to the center by God / Gene Robinson.
      p. cm.
    Includes bibliographical references and index.
    ISBN 978-1-59627-088-6 (casebound w/ jacket : alk. paper)
    1. Robinson, V. Gene, 1947- 2. Episcopal Church – New Hampshire – Clergy – Biography. 3. Episcopal Church – Bishops – Appointment, call, and election. 4. Gay clergy – New Hampshire – Biography. 5. Homosexuality – Religious aspects – Anglican Communion. 6. Homosexuality – Religious aspects – Episcopal Church. 7. Church work – Anglican Communion. 8. Church work – Episcopal Church. 9. Anglican Communion – Forecasting. 10. Episcopal Church – Forecasting. I. Title.
BX5995.R56A3 2008
283.092 – dc22
[B]   2008002052

Printed in the United States of America

08 09 10 11 12 13 14 15   8 7 6 5 4 3 2 1

Because this book is not just about what I think, but who I am, I want to give thanks for those who have played such an important role in my journey:

This book is for my parents, Victor and Imogene, who first taught me about God's love, and my sister, Karen, whose support has never wavered; for the people of the Diocese of New Hampshire, who continue to shape and support me; for Tim Rich, my friend, colleague and soulmate; for Bishop Doug Theuner, my predecessor and friend, the earliest one to see my sexuality as no impediment to ministry; for Paula Bibber, without whom my life and schedule would be chaos; for Barbara Harris, the first woman bishop and my role model and hero; for Tom Ely, brother bishop and friend, on whom I depend for godly wisdom and counsel; for Jim Johnson, Paul Hokemeyer, and Blake Franklin, without whom my wider ministry would not be possible; for "Boo" McDaniel, my former wife, for the marriage we shared and for her support that continues to this day; for Daniel Karslake and Russ Anderson and the joyous and exciting four years we have shared; for Bonnie and Glen Anderson and their three decades of love and support; for the friends, each with more than twenty years of love under their belts, who continue to inspire us — Bruce and Barry, Steve and Don, Mary and Nancy, Mary and Sue, Tim and James; and, of course, for my beloved Mark, Jamee, and Ella.

Contents

Part Three
EMBRACING THE EXILE
Notes from the Margins

Part Four
GOD'S LOVING HANDS IN THE WORLD
Building the Body of Christ

Part Five
THE COMPASS ROSE
Charting the Course of the Anglican Communion

FOREWORD

I HAVE BEEN PUZZLED by a strange fact — that a largely conservative, rural small-town diocese such as New Hampshire
should have elected a man in an open, monogamous relationship
with another man. It just did not make sense that they would
want to run the gauntlet of controversy, opprobrium, and turmoil for the sheer heck of it. Having read Bishop Gene Robinson's
manuscript of this book I now know why. They had as one of the
candidates at the Diocesan Convention to elect their bishop a man
many had come to know quite well, and they had been impressed
with what they had seen and experienced of him.

He was, he still is, a man with an all-consuming passion, and
that is to proclaim the Gospel of Jesus Christ, to assure as many as
will hear him of their infinite worth in the sight of God who loved
them and still loves them with a love that is unconditional and
that will not let them go. Gene Robinson has the heart of a pastor, compassionate and deeply caring for each person whatever
that person's condition. He tells so movingly of the Christmas
present he gives himself every year since becoming bishop. On
Christmas Eve he goes to the New Hampshire State Prison for
Women, and he has endeared himself so much to these inmates
that they embroidered a set of vestments on the inside of which
they stitched their names. This Advent vestment set is his favorite
among his ecclesiastical garb. He has given the women prisoners
hope. (Advent is the liturgical season of hope, of expectancy, of
longing for the coming of the Christ as Judge as he came as an infant, a coming we commemorate each Christmas.) Poignantly for
these women it is a time of expectancy, of hope — hope of parole,

of release, of a visit from a loved one. Their bishop, who came dressed to the ecclesiastical nines in all his consecration regalia when he first visited them — to affirm their significance for him and hopefully for themselves — reflects the character of Christ the Good Shepherd who gave up, who gives up on no one.

He has wanted to live out his life as an *alter Christus,* another Christ, proclaiming the love of a father longing eagerly for the return of his wayward younger son whom he rushes out to embrace when he does return, even before he has confessed his wrongdoing. He has wanted to be where Christ would be — among the down and outs, the lost, the last, the least.

It is these attributes that have attracted people. It is these qualities that made the people of the Diocese of New Hampshire elect him thereby provoking a massive ecclesiastical storm. This is the man they knew, and this is the man they chose to be their father-in-God. They would not recognize him in the caricatures that make out that he is consumed by one issue and that being this nettle of the acceptance of lgbt persons in the church as full members free to enjoy all the rights and privileges and benefits that heterosexual members enjoy. But this is not his obsession. He cares about other issues of public concern, such as the Iraq War, such as the erosion of citizens' rights in the wake of the deep anxiety and fear that have characterized U.S. politics.

I have met him only once and I was impressed by his demeanor and presence. For someone in the eye of the storm buffeting our beloved Anglican Communion, he is so serene; he is not a wild-eyed belligerent campaigner. I was so surprised at his generosity towards those who have denigrated him and worse. After all, he and his partner had to wear bulletproof vests for his consecration. He has received death threats — all of which ought to have made him want to give as much as he had got. No, he is not vengeful. I have been amazed at his magnanimity, which reminded me so much of the generosity of spirit that was displayed by many of the victims who came to testify before the

South African Truth and Reconciliation Commission. We were frequently bowled over by the incredible willingness to forgive of many who had suffered grievously at the hands of perpetrators of gruesome atrocities. Instead of baying for their blood as might have been expected, they chose to walk the path of forgiveness and reconciliation rather than that of retribution and revenge. They did not demonize their adversary. By their act of forgiveness they set themselves free from the bondage of victimhood, and they gave the perpetrator the opportunity, if he wanted to accept it, of making a new beginning.

Gene Robinson, breathtakingly, says of those opposing him who have been vituperative and worse that they are all, including him, destined for heaven. He has refused to demonize them. After all the calumny heaped on him he might have been forgiven for hoping that his adversaries would end up in the warmer place. Our Lord must smile to have such a splendid representative in an affair that has often been sordid.

He is so utterly irenic, and his hermeneutics — his manner of understanding the scriptures as being time-bound and thus conditioned by cultural language, beliefs, contemporary knowledge, etc. — is so reasonable and persuasive.

For me, the question of human sexuality is really a matter of justice; of course I would be willing to show that my beliefs are not inconsistent with how we have come to understand the scriptures. It is not enough to say the "Bible says...," for the Bible says many things that I find totally unacceptable and indeed abhorrent. I accept the authority of the Bible as the Word of God, but I remember that the Bible has been used to justify racism, slavery, and the humiliation of women, etc. Apartheid was supported by the white Dutch Reformed Church in South Africa, which claimed that there was biblical sanction for that vicious system.

Many of us were engaged in the anti-apartheid struggle. Apartheid, crassly racist, sought to penalize people for something about which they could do nothing — their ethnicity, their skin color. Most of the world agreed that that was unacceptable, that it was unjust.

I joined the many who campaigned against an injustice that the church tolerated in its ranks when women were not allowed to be ordained. They were being penalized for something about which they could do nothing, their gender. Mercifully that is no longer the case in our Province of the Anglican Communion, and how enriched we have been by this move.

I could not stand by while people were being penalized again for something about which they could do nothing — their sexual orientation. I am humbled and honored to stand shoulder to shoulder with those who seek to end this egregious wrong inflicted on God's children.

May I wholly inadequately apologize to my sisters and brothers who are gay, lesbian, bisexual, or transgendered for the cruelty and injustice that you have suffered and continue to suffer at the hands of us, your fellow Anglicans; I am sorry. Forgive us for all the pain we have caused you and which we continue to inflict on you.

Gene Robinson is a wonderful human being, and I am proud to belong to the same church as he.

Desmond Tutu
Capetown, South Africa
January 8, 2008

INTRODUCTION

A T JUST BEFORE eleven o'clock in the morning, on Saturday, June 7, 2003, my life irrevocably changed. Prior to that moment, I was just me — a priest of some thirty years, a father, a partner and son, and a follower of Christ. From that early-summer moment on, although I didn't understand or comprehend it at the time, my life would never be the same again.

It was never clear to me that I'd become a bishop of the Episcopal Church. What I did know, as best as I could discern it, was that God wanted me to allow my name to go forward in episcopal elections. I supposed it was just to get the church to deal more openly and honestly with its gay and lesbian members. I hoped doing this would at least open the conversation about the full inclusion of lesbian, gay, bisexual, and transgendered people in the life and leadership of the church.

The atmosphere at St. Paul's Church, Concord, on that summer morning was electric. The Holy Spirit seemed so palpably present that people spoke of the hair standing up on their necks. While the first ballots were being counted, you could have heard a pin drop, as people sat silently or knelt humbly in prayer. When the final result was read, announcing my election as the ninth Bishop of New Hampshire, a rush of wind swept through the congregation as people rose to their feet to applaud, cheer, laugh, cry, and rejoice. People who were there still refer to it as one of the most moving and powerful experiences of God in their lifetimes.

What followed could only be described as a storm — to some, the perfect storm. My election focused a debate that had already

1

begun about "two churches" within the Episcopal Church, a debate that had begun with the ordination of women nearly thirty years before. The storm continued at the 2003 General Convention of the Episcopal Church, where a majority of laity, clergy, and bishops would be asked to give consent to my election.

During that consent process, scurrilous charges of sexual misconduct and linkage to a pornographic website were brought forward in an effort to derail the church's consent to my election. While those charges were being investigated, as I was sequestered away in my hotel room with my partner and daughter, the priest who would later become my Canon to the Ordinary brought me a piece of calligraphy that read: "Sometimes God calms the storm. And sometimes God lets the storm rage and calms his child." A day or two later, I received a photograph from a fellow priest of the diocese — a weather satellite photo taken miles above a huge hurricane in the Atlantic. In the center of that terrible and fierce storm was a tiny pinpoint of blue calm. That is where I have tried to put myself ever since my life changed.

But the fact of the matter is that I cannot live in the eye of the storm on my own. I can't get myself there or keep myself there. Only God can bring me to that place of peace and sustain me there. Only God can calm and soothe me when hatred and vitriol come my way. Only God can persuade me not to step into the powerful winds swirling about me; when I do, only God can keep me from being swept away by their destructive power.

Whatever mistakes I've made in these early years of my episcopate, I am to blame. Whatever good I might have achieved or inspired, God is the reason. I have not gotten all this right, nor will I. But God has been very clear with me that whether I get it all right or not, I am his. Or as I often say to the people of my diocese, "When all is said and done, you and I are going to heaven." And in comparison to that, everything else is small potatoes.

In my election, God seems to have done what God has always done: taken the least likely and least worthy persons and attempted to do extraordinary things through them. As Jesus reached out to the margins of his own society, to touch and save and empower lepers, prostitutes, tax collectors, and all sorts of the marginalized, so God has reached out to the margins of our society and called one of God's gay children to serve in this special way, at this most difficult time. It probably sounds arrogant to say it, but it *is* the way I've experienced it. I could be completely wrong — only time will tell — but I believe that I have indeed been "swept to the center by God." Swept from the margins into the center of the storm — for God's purposes and to accomplish God's will. God is big in this, and I am small. God's purposes are trustworthy and pure, while mine are faulty and all-too-human. But God has made the outrageous promise to take our wills and mold them according to his, to provide us with what we need in order to do God's will, and to be with us to the ends of the earth. Without that promise and without God's constant and ever-close presence, I could not have withstood the storm of the last five years.

Since my election and consecration as Bishop of New Hampshire in 2003, one thing has troubled me most: the characterization of me by the press, the public, and the Anglican Communion as a single-issue, one-dimensional person. In the first fifty-six years of my life, I think I was known as a passionate preacher and communicator of the Gospel, lived out in my ministry as a parish priest, retreat center founder/director, program coordinator for the seven dioceses of New England, and assistant to the Bishop of New Hampshire. But since my election, you'd surmise from press reports that the only thing I care about is the inclusion of gay, lesbian, bisexual, and transgendered Christians in the church. While I do indeed care deeply about that issue, it's only one part of my larger, more important passion: the saving grace of a God who loves us beyond our wildest imagining and who revealed himself in the life, death, and resurrection of Jesus Christ. God has taken this drastic action so that we *all* might be free of the sin that paralyses us and keeps us from being all that God wants us to be. And why? For the reconciliation and redemption of the world.

I was persuaded to write this book because it would allow me to talk about my real passion: the Gospel of Jesus Christ, the good news that we are loved by the God who created us, and, through our redemption by Jesus on the cross, that we are set free to love one another and the world in God's Name. That liberation is for gay and lesbian people, of course, who are children of God and whose souls are just as important to save as other souls. But that liberation is also for every single one of God's children.

It might surprise readers (I hope it will) to learn just how "orthodox" I am. Perhaps both my supporters *and* my critics will be surprised at just how theologically conservative I am. Just because I favor taking a second look at what holy scripture actually says — and doesn't say — about homosexuality as we understand it today, it doesn't follow that I believe everything in scripture is up for grabs. I have listened long and hard to my conservative brothers and sisters in Christ when they express their fears that those of us who favor the full inclusion and participation of gay and lesbian people in the life and leadership of the Episcopal Church also favor the deconstruction of orthodox doctrines such as the Trinity and the divinity of Christ. The fear that inclusion of lgbt folk in the church is but a precursor to an all-out attack on the long-held orthodox doctrines of the church may be our greatest stumbling block to full inclusion. My hope is that this book will speak to those fears in a way that sets the acceptance of gay and lesbian Christians within the larger context of orthodox belief.

My life as a bishop, spending most of my time doing the myriad yet unremarkable things a bishop does, would not normally permit me the time to write a book. I've been, however, enabled to do so because of two enormous blessings: a sabbatical leave given to me by my beloved diocese and an editor, Nancy Fitzgerald, who helped me shape this book. I am grateful for this opportunity to share my passion for the Gospel in this broader context.

First and foremost, this book is dedicated to the glory of God, who continues to bring Easters out of the Good Fridays of my life. If this book points to me, rather than to God, it would be better if I'd never written it.

This book is dedicated to the people of my diocese. The privilege of having been called by them to serve as their bishop is indescribable. I've never received a greater honor from brother and sister Christians, and to be so honored by the people I had already served for twenty-eight years is a profoundly humbling experience. I can never hope to live up to that great calling, but I am committed, for as long as I have, to being as faithful as I can be to it. In some small way, I hope this book will reveal to the world why the people of the Diocese of New Hampshire might have seen me as fit material for the episcopate, not, as has often been assumed, that the diocese was trying to make a political statement, but rather that they sought a known companion on the journey of faith to lead them into the future.

This book is dedicated to my parents, Victor and Imogene Robinson, who have loved me "no matter what." Coming to know that their son is gay was a terrible and almost unbearable shock to them more than twenty years ago. The journey they've made to acceptance is nothing short of miraculous — and is yet another testimony to the God of love, about whom I first learned from them.

This book is dedicated to my daughters, Jamee and Ella, whose love has been as steady and true as any father could ever hope for. Their love, humor, and devotion have sustained and nurtured me all along the way. And it is in the hope for a better world for my granddaughters, Morgan and Megan, that I do this work.

Lastly, and most deeply, this book is dedicated to my partner, Mark. Little did either of us know twenty years ago where our life together would lead, but I am eternally grateful for his willingness to make the trip. Because he is a private person, such a life in the spotlight is Mark's idea of a nightmare — and yet he has been not only willing, but fully supportive of this journey, which has changed both our lives. Along with me, he too has found a new ministry in God's name. Our home is a safe harbor, and his quiet steadiness and faithful support is my anchor in the storm.

Part One

THE ELEPHANT IN THE ROOM

Homosexuality and the Church

O God, you made us in your own image and redeemed us through Jesus your Son: Look with compassion on the whole human family; take away the arrogance and hatred which infect our hearts; break down the walls that separate us; unite us in bonds of love; and work through our struggle and confusion to accomplish your purposes on earth; that, in your good time, all nations and races may serve you in harmony around your heavenly throne; through Jesus Christ our Lord. Amen. —Prayer for the Human Family, The Book of Common Prayer, page 815

MANY WALLS separate us from one another: poverty, disease, race, gender, prejudice, and fear of the other. But the wall that occupies much of our time and energy now is the one that excludes lesbian, gay, bisexual, and transgendered people from the wider community of Christians. Passionate conversations, on both sides of the wall, debate whether or not God's loving embrace includes and affirms lgbt people, and whether or not they have a rightful place in the life and ordained leadership of the church.

This has become an issue for the church because in recent years huge numbers of people, many of them faithful and active Episcopalians, have "come out" to their families, friends, neighbors, and brothers and sisters in Christ. For the first time in history, we can no longer talk about "them," as if they were a strange and foreign subset of abnormal people, but rather we have had to acknowledge that they are "us." What's the church to do?

* 1 *

A MIGHTY WIND

This is a story about Pentecost Sunday. A priest in a large church in Florida, with his usual flair for the dramatic, decided to dramatize the Holy Spirit coming like wind in a particularly spectacular way. He got the engine out of one of the boats used in the Everglades — an airplane propeller attached to a big gasoline engine — and mounted it in the choir loft high in the back of the church. The wind from the propeller would blow out across the congregation when the story of the coming of the Holy Spirit was read. It seemed like a great idea.

The priest and an usher gave it a dry run on Saturday afternoon, and although it was incredibly noisy, it worked just fine, and promised a spectacular effect for Sunday morning. So when the great moment arrived, and the lector read, "And suddenly from heaven there came a sound like the rush of a violent wind and it filled the entire house," the engine coughed once and then howled into life.

But the effect was a little different than it had been at rehearsal. The sudden screaming gust of wind sent sheet music and bulletins flying out over the congregation. Coiffures came undone and hair streamed out from faces. The preacher's sermon notes were gone with the wind. A hairpiece flew toward the altar like a furry missile. It was like a scene from the play "Green Pastures," when the Angel Gabriel looks down from heaven and says to the Lord, "Everything that was nailed down is comin' loose!"

Everything was messy, and noisy, and absolutely unpredictable. And that's just the way it is with the Spirit. It's that part of God that refuses to be contained in the little boxes we create for God to live in, safely confined to the careful boundaries we set for God's Spirit. The problem is — and the miracle is — God just won't stay put. And God won't let you and me stay put, content to believe what we've always believed, what we've always been taught, what we've always assumed. Change isn't just something to be wished on our enemies — but something God requires of us as well.

Think of the things we believe and think today that we couldn't have imagined years ago. There was a time when we weren't outraged that black folk were made to drink from separate water fountains, that women were banned from serving at the altar or the boardroom, that differently abled folk couldn't get into our sacred spaces. Our change in thinking didn't come as a result of our own work, but the work of God's Spirit, blowing through us like wind, calling us away from our narrow thinking and more nearly into the mind and heart of Christ.

Remember how the church thought of gay men and lesbians, bisexual and transgendered people — and more importantly think of the way they understood themselves. They believed the church when they were told that they were an abomination before God. They believed the church when they were told that their relationships — indeed their lives — were intrinsically disordered, that they were second-class hangers-on in the church of God, loved perhaps, but "only if.... "

And then the Spirit of God blew through us like a mighty wind. We heard God's calm and loving voice above the noisy din of the church's condemnation. And we were saved, made worthy to stand before God through Christ's sacrifice on the cross. Quite literally, we were "born again," and our lives were changed forever. Think of the joy we've come to know because of the Spirit's work within us.

This life-changing work of the Spirit has been going on for a long, long time. St. Peter was horrified, in his dream about eating "unclean" food, to hear God saying, "Don't be so picky about what people eat! Care more about what's in their hearts. My Word is broader and deeper than that, and I am going to be calling people unto me whom you have thought were unacceptable in my eyes. But you've been wrong, and I'm going to show you a different way."

Is there any doubt in your mind that the Holy Spirit is alive and well, even now, and calling the church to open itself to all those whom Jesus loves? We don't worship a God who is all locked up in scripture two thousand years ago, but a God whose love knows no human bounds. The Spirit of God longs for, yearns for, and even demands that there cease to be "us" and "them."

God calls us to the hard work of compassion for our enemies. Some people may quarrel with that characterization, but we do have enemies. It's a word that Jesus used. The hard part is following Jesus' own command to love our enemies. Not to like them, not to be paralyzed by their opposition, not to give in to their outrageous demands, but to love them nevertheless. To treat them with infinite respect, listen to what drives them, try our best to understand the fear that causes them to reject us, to believe them when they say they only want the best for us. That's hard work, and we can't do it without God's own Spirit blowing through us like wind, breaking down our walls, causing our assumptions to "come loose," and reminding us that our enemies too are children of God, for whom Christ died and through whom they will be saved.

So what are we to do? Let's return to the stories of the first-century church and its witness, which ultimately brings us here as the church of the twenty-first century. Look at what our ancestors in the faith did. They didn't denigrate their enemies; they didn't doubt that their enemies were children of God. Rather, they spoke of God's love for themselves and what Jesus Christ had done in their own lives, breaking loose the bondage of sin and death that keeps us all from the abundant life promised by the Savior. By word and example, our Christian ancestors proclaimed what God had done in their lives, and then they let the Spirit do the rest.

Our job is the same as it's always been for Christians: to proclaim with boldness and clarity not what we have done, but what God has done in and through us. Our lives must be lived with such joy and vibrancy and trust in God that all will come to see that we are indeed, along with all of humanity, children of the Most High. That will be the only thing that will change hearts. It's the only thing that ever has.

Here's a question I've been asked countless times: "How do you do what you do? How do you seem calm and loving, even when insults are coming your way, even when holy scripture is being flung in your face like mud?" This is my secret: it comes from the "other book" (besides the Bible) that changed my life. I can pinpoint the moment in my life when my ministry changed and I became willing to lose everything for the Gospel and for Jesus who is the Word.

The book is *Embracing the Exile,* by John Fortunato. John went through a bruising, nasty, and very public ordeal when he and his partner tried to have their relationship blessed in their local Episcopal parish — many years before such things were publicly contemplated. He endured all the hatred and vitriol you might expect that such an event would incur in the world and church of the 1980s.

In the opening and closing chapters of his book, he describes getting up in the middle of a sleepless night, in pain over the abuse heaped on him by Christians and non-Christians alike for loving another man and wanting the church's blessing on their relationship. Sitting alone in the dark, he had a vision. Or was it his imagination? Or an epiphany? Whatever it was, God was right there. John describes it this way:

I was saying, "You know, sometimes I think they're right, that being gay and loving a man is wrong." God smiled and said quietly, "How can love be wrong? It all comes from me."

"Sometimes, I just want to bury that part of me," I said, "just pretend it isn't real."

"But I made you whole," God replied. "You are one as I am one. I made you in my image."

"*Your* church out there says that you don't love me. They say that I'm lost, damned to hell."

"You're my son," God said in a way both gentle and yet so firm that there could be no doubt of his genuineness. "Nothing can separate you from my love...."

"What do I do with *them?*"

And in the same calm voice, God said, "I've given you gifts. Share them. I've given you light. Brighten the world. I empower you with my love. Love them."

"*Love* them? What are you trying to do to me? Can't you see? They call my light darkness! They call my love perverted! They call my gifts corruptions! What the hell are you asking me to do?"

"Love them anyway," he said. "Love them anyway."

"Love them anyway?" I moaned. "But how?"

"...you must also speak your pain and affirm the wholeness I've made you to be when they assail it. You must protest when you are treated as less than a child of mine. You must go out and teach them. Help them to know of their dependence on me for all that they really are, and of their helplessness without me.... And assure them by word and work and example that my love is boundless, and that I am with them always."

"You know they won't listen to me," I said with resignation. "They'll despise me. They'll call me a heretic and laugh me to scorn. They'll persecute and torment me. They'll try to destroy me. You know they will, don't you."

[God's] radiant face saddened. And then God said softly, "Oh, yes. I know. How well I know."

Then two strong, motherly arms reached out and drew me close to the bosom of all that is. And I was just there. Just being. Enveloped in being.

And we wept.

For joy.[1]

That's it. That's the entire story. All we are asked to do, by the God of all creation, is to "love them anyway." No matter what gets said, no matter what laws get passed or not, no matter how soon or how long it takes for us to find justice, we already have God's love. And all we are asked to do is to "love them anyway." *All* of them. And trust God — and God's Spirit, blowing like a mighty wind — to do the rest.

---

1. John E. Fortunato, *Embracing the Exile: Healing Journeys of Gay Christians* (New York: Seabury, 1982), 15–16, 126–27.

❋ 2 ❋

CIVIL DISCOURSE

Sometimes — who knows why — the world just seems to be ready for a movement or a cause. In our day, it's full civil rights for gay, lesbian, bisexual, and transgendered people. But swirling around this movement is a galaxy of questions. Why are we here in this particular moment, struggling with this particular issue? Why does religion play a central role in this debate — and is that role appropriate in public discourse? Who are the loudest, strongest voices coming from the religious community, and why are they so strident, unrelenting, and passionate? What does the Bible *really* say about homosexuality, what does it not say, and why does it matter in a secular state? What is the rightful role of religion in public discourse? How does this debate about the civil rights of lgbt people relate to the other "isms" of our culture, and what is the broader context for discussion of human rights for all citizens? How do we move forward in the never-ending search for the common good?

What the answers are depends on who you are. Look at me. Let's just note for the record that I am male. I will never know what it's like to live my life as a female, and if a lesbian were writing this, her perspective would be entirely different. I am a white man. The experience of being gay in a community of color is different than mine, too, especially since gay people of color experience a double discrimination that I can only imagine. I grew up in a family that was poor, uneducated, and deeply religious, in a rural, largely segregated region of Kentucky, where we were tobacco tenant farmers, living without running water or central heat, but unaware of how poor we were. All of that colors who I was, who I came to be, and how I understand my own story. Not in my wildest dreams did I ever imagine a world in which we'd be talking openly about homosexuality, much less having an international debate in which I'd sometimes, reluctantly, find myself at the center.

I am a Christian. The fact that I am tempted to add "but not *that* kind of Christian" speaks to the powerful role the conservative Religious Right has come to play in this debate. While I believe Jesus of Nazareth is the Messiah, I don't believe he is the sole revelation of God's self to the world. I respect and revere all those who have come to know God through other faith journeys. I can only speak out of my own context as a Christian, and I trust others to make the connections and translations into the understandings of their own faith communities. After all, the challenge before us as citizens of democracies is to define our rights and responsibilities to one another no matter what our beliefs are.

Why are we here in this particular moment in the history of this country and in the struggle for human rights? In the 1970s, most North Americans, like most Britons or Australians, would have told you — honestly — that they didn't know any gay or lesbian people. If pushed, they might admit that there was weird Uncle Harry, a lifelong bachelor who everyone knew was a bit different, or those two spinster ladies who'd lived together down the street for as long as anyone could remember. But did they know any out, proud, and self-affirming gay and lesbian people? Probably not.

Fast-forward to today. Is there anyone left who doesn't know a family member, co-worker, or neighbor who is gay? The reason, of course, is that the intervening decades have seen the unprecedented efforts of gay and lesbian people to make themselves known — as gay and lesbian — to their families, co-workers, and friends. Progress, of course, has proceeded at differing rates based on geography and culture. Metropolitan areas, to which many gay and lesbian people have gravitated because of both anonymity and generally more liberal attitudes, were the vanguard of these public admissions of sexual orientation, and these more secular, less religious, settings have provided more open and accepting environments for coming out. But the real shift in the culture has been the quiet, mostly private admissions by sons and daughters, cousins and aunts and uncles, in families from Birmingham to Boise, from Liverpool to Chipping Norton, from Winnipeg to Sydney: "Yes, I too am gay."

It was the countless dramas, played out one at a time, of gay and lesbian people, courageously sharing who they really were at the core of their being with those they loved or worked with, that have literally changed the world and brought us to this moment.

That's the way change always happens. You have a worldview that seems to work pretty well at interpreting reality — then bam! Something happens that doesn't fit into that view, something that your old worldview can't even explain. You're thrown into chaos and confusion, and nothing seems certain anymore. And then, little by little, your old worldview is reshaped to accommodate this new truth.

That's the way it happens for families of gay and lesbian people. Parents believe the traditional view that homosexuals are immoral, sick, disordered, and misguided — until a beloved child comes and says, "Mom, Dad, I'm gay." The parents are plunged, on the one hand, into the chaos of knowing their beloved children are *not* immoral, sick, disordered, or misguided, and on the other hand, knowing that's what's been said about gay people by the church and the world. Over time, they come to understand that their children are exactly the same people they've always been, only happier and healthier. The old worldview about homosexuality is overhauled into a new understanding that allows parents to continue loving their children. They may not be out there beating the drum for marriage equality (although many of them are), and they may not be bragging to all their friends about their son's new boyfriend (though some of them may), but something deep and important has changed, some significant piece of ground has shifted, and the world isn't the same as it was. That is happening all over the world at any given moment.

Around the globe nations, cultures, and religions are dealing with the issue of homosexuality. Even those religions that are absolutely clear and unswerving in their condemnation of homosexuality are being challenged by their gay and lesbian members to take another look at that condemnation. Some estimate, for example, that between 40 and 60 percent of Roman Catholic priests are gay.[1] The Southern Baptist Convention, to which local autonomy is almost sacred, has expelled congregations for offering blessings to same-sex couples or for calling a gay minister. Conservative Jews have admitted gay and lesbian, bisexual, and transgendered rabbinical students to their seminaries. Evangelical Christians have been rocked by revelations that some of their leaders have had secret affairs with people of the same sex.

Who'd have thought we'd ever see legal civil unions and even marriage for gay and lesbian couples? Who'd have thought that a country like South Africa would write gay and lesbian civil rights explicitly into its constitution, or that a Roman Catholic country like Spain would permit marriage between same-sex couples? Many Anglicans from around the world continue to call on me to resign my position as bishop, naively believing that if I went away, this issue would go away, and the church would return to its quiet, peaceful existence — though the church has never, in its two-thousand-year history, enjoyed a time free of conflict.

Why does religion play such an important role in this debate? Religion, of course, has always played a role in the public discourse of nations. But why the particularly virulent and passionate stances on this issue? And why can't we simply ignore the religious argument and have a thoroughly secular debate?

---

1. Elizabeth Stuart, *Chosen: Gay Catholic Priests Tell Their Stories* (London and New York: Chapman, 1993).

Religion makes its beliefs known on a variety of issues — from abortion to stem cell research, from environmental stewardship to capital punishment. But most faith communities have people on both sides of these issues within their ranks — at least in part because you can't find too many definite proclamations in scripture either for or against them. You can read Genesis 1:28, for instance ("Be fruitful and multiply, and fill the earth and subdue it; and have dominion over the fish of the sea and over the birds of the air and over every living thing that moves upon the earth"), and argue for good environmental stewardship. Or using the same verse but different understandings of key words, you can argue for total exploitation of the environment. You can defend abortion on the basis of our God-given personal conscience or oppose it on the basis of the sanctity of life.

But the Bible doesn't seem to mince any words about homosexuality. Leviticus, for instance, seems specifically to condemn male homosexuality: "You [men] shall not lie with a male as with a woman; it is an abomination" (18:22) and "If a man lies with a male as with a woman, both of them have committed an abomination; they shall be put to death" (20:13). (There are no same-sex proscriptions for women in these texts, by the way.) The fact that the Bible seems specifically to name homosexuality as repugnant to God and worthy of capital punishment makes religion particularly relevant to our understanding of this issue, in ways that are more compelling than with other hot-button issues.

The fact is, at least in Western culture, God's condemnation of homosexuality is assumed. It's in the air we breathe. And because of that, religious belief *is* relevant in our discourse about civil rights for gay and lesbian people.

So what does the Bible *really* say about homosexuality? I believe our traditional understanding of the biblical — hence God's — attitude toward homosexuals is flawed and needs to be reinterpreted.

First, the philosophical and psychological construct of sexual orientation is a modern phenomenon. It was only at the very end of the nineteenth century that the notion was first posed that there might be a certain minority of people who are naturally oriented — affectionally and sexually — toward members of the same gender. In biblical times, and until the last hundred or so years, it's been assumed that everyone is heterosexual, which meant that anyone acting in a homosexual manner was acting "against their nature." In other words, homosexuals were "heterosexuals behaving badly." Indeed, many recent evangelical translations of the Bible use the word "homosexual" to translate certain Greek and Hebrew words that may not be related to homosexuality per se, but to sexual exploitation and abuse of underage boys by older men, common in Roman and Greek culture, and to temple prostitution in neighboring heathen cultures. Yet reading one of these translations using the word "homosexual," you'd assume that the ancient Hebrew and Christian communities were talking about precisely the same thing we're talking about today. That's not the case. You can't take a twentieth-century word, insert it back into an ancient text, and proclaim that it means something totally unknown to the authors of that text.

Second, our understanding of the word "abomination" is different from its original use. According to the Holiness Code in the Book of Leviticus, many things were an "abomination" to God, including the eating of pork. Eating pork wasn't innately wrong, but abstaining from it was one of the ways Jews were reminded that they were a separate, chosen people. Observing the dietary laws reminded them of this special relationship to God. Jews were also forbidden to eat shellfish, plant two kinds of seed in the same field, or wear two kinds of cloth simultaneously. Tattoos were prohibited; those who cursed their parents were to be put to death. Yet you don't hear leaders from the Religious Right denouncing these "abominations."

Third, the ancient Hebrews' understanding of the science of reproduction and sexual activity was different from ours today. Male sperm was thought to contain all of nascent life; the only contribution made by women in the reproductive process was providing a place for the fetus to incubate. So any "spilling" of male seed was considered tantamount to murder. Ancient Hebrews were a small minority, living in a hostile, heathen environment, struggling to reproduce, build up their population, and survive, so any waste of male sperm was antithetical to that survival and synonymous with not only murder, but a betrayal of the national interest. In the same way, masturbation and even coitus interruptus in heterosexual copulation (the so-called "sin of Onan") were prohibited because they wasted male seed and squandered the possibility of new human life. Today, we understand that both sexes contribute to the process of human reproduction, and our day's problem is over-population rather than under-population. We believe sexuality to have purposes far beyond reproduction. Yet these few verses of scripture are quoted as if nothing has changed in our understanding since biblical times. Note, of course, that all the other references to the "spilling of seed" have been reinterpreted to be acceptable, but not the proscription against same-sex behavior.

Recent studies have yielded rich information about the culture in which these texts were written and heard. Much of the biblical scholarship of the past fifty years has focused on the societies and cultures that formed the settings for these scriptural texts, both those of the ancient Hebrews and those of the early Christians, as well as the competing and often hostile cultures surrounding them. We've come to know the deeper meaning of these sacred texts as we've become more knowledgeable about the cultural situations to which they were responses. Those who argue for a literalist reading of scripture often act as if none of this scholarship has occurred or makes any difference to a twenty-first-century understanding.

And though I believe the holy scriptures of the Old and New Testaments are the Word of God, that doesn't mean they are literally the "words" of God, virtually dictated by God through human media. And let's not forget that the real "Word" of God is Jesus himself. "In the beginning was the Word, and the Word was with God, and the Word was God," begins the Gospel of John. Christians believe it isn't the Bible but the Jesus "event" — his life, death, and resurrection — that offers the perfect revelation of God. The Bible is the best and most trustworthy witness to that event, but it neither replaces Jesus as the Word nor takes precedence over Christ's continuing action in the world through the Holy Spirit. To elevate the words of scripture to a place higher than the revealed Word of God in Jesus Christ is an act of idolatry.

These things may seem hopelessly off-topic for issues related to gay and lesbian people, but they're all deeply related. We're talking about how we change our minds — as a culture, a nation, and a church — about something we've been very sure about for thousands of years. To some, it seems like the height of madness and a willy-nilly discarding of ancient truths. To some, it seems as if nothing is certain anymore, or that the church doesn't know *what* it believes. But to others, it seems like the kind of change that Jesus promised would be inspired by the Holy Spirit. Only through such a gentle and comforting understanding of the continuing work of God will people find the courage to change their minds about this issue.

But why is the resistance to change on this issue so vehement, so vitriolic, so deep? Why would two people wanting to pledge their love and fidelity to one another for their mutual benefit and the benefit of society be seen as a problem? Why wouldn't conservatives applaud the pledge of faithful monogamy in gay marriage for the people they've always accused of being promiscuous and irresponsible? Why wouldn't conservative Christians want to see gay people stop entering usually disastrous heterosexual marriages just to be happy and accepted? Why can conservatives use gay marriage as an effective wedge issue in political campaigns?

Or in the church, why would my election as bishop of a fairly conservative, rural, and small-town diocese in New England turn into a worldwide controversy? How could my election spawn thousands of hateful letters and emails? Why would I, a Christian elected by the clergy and people of a diocese to be their bishop, receive death threats from other religious people and have to wear a bulletproof vest for my consecration? Why would people around the world, from the bush of Kenya to the remotest of Pacific islands, debate my fitness for this calling, based not on my skills, experience, and faithfulness, but on my sexual orientation? Why would some leaders in the Anglican Communion consider it dangerous to meet with me, talk with me, or even be seen with me?

First, we've never been very comfortable talking about sex. The Puritans in American culture didn't help, nor did the Victorian Age in Britain, with its often duplicitous sensibilities. The realities of our sexual lives are perhaps too frightening to bring to the light of day.

Yet many of the moral issues that face us today involve sexuality. Abortion, fertility therapies, alternative methods of re-production, the role of men and women, and the ending of half of all marriages in divorce that signals a crisis for the contemporary family — all these involve sexuality. We need to talk about these things, yet we have little experience doing so. Parents still falter over what to tell their children about sex — and when. Perhaps our near-obsession with homosexuality is a group denial mechanism for heterosexuals not to talk about their own sexual issues. If we can talk about *them*, then we don't have to talk about *us*. If we can focus on *their* problems, we don't have to talk about our own.

Most people resist seeing the treatment of homosexuals as "their" problem. Gay and lesbian people have known for a long time that the problem isn't gay and lesbian people's sexuality, but their ill treatment by a hostile society.

The problem, though, isn't exactly "homophobia." That surely exists, but it's always a conversation stopper. Some claim they're not afraid of homosexuals so they're "not guilty" of homophobia. But the further sin our society is guilty of is "heterosexism."

Everyone knows what an "ism" is: a set of prejudices and values and judgments backed up with the power to enforce those prejudices in society. Racism isn't just fear and loathing of nonwhite people; it's the systemic network of laws, customs, and beliefs that perpetuate prejudicial treatment of people of color. I benefit every day from being white in this culture. I don't have to hate anyone, or call anyone a hateful name, or do any harm to a person of color to benefit from a racist society. I just have to sit back and reap the rewards of a system set up to benefit me. I can even be tolerant, open-minded, and multi-culturally sensitive. But as long as I'm not working to dismantle the system, I am racist.

Similarly, sexism isn't just the denigration and devaluation of women; it's the myriad ways the system is set up to benefit men over women. It takes no hateful behavior on my part to reap the rewards given to men at the expense of women. But to choose *not* to work for the full equality of women in this culture is to be sexist.

So the sin we're fighting now, within the secular sphere, is the sin of heterosexism. More and more people are feeling kindly toward gay and lesbian people, but that will never be enough. More important is the dismantling of the system that rewards heterosexuals at the expense of homosexuals. That's why equal marriage rights are so important. That's why "don't ask, don't tell" is such a failure and such a painful thing for gay and lesbian people, even those who have no desire to serve in the military. These are ever-present reminders that our identities, our lives, and our relationships are second class — because the very system of laws that govern us discriminates against us and denigrates our lives.

At their root, heterosexism and homophobia are expressions of misogyny, the hatred of women. If you doubt the currency of this misogynistic attitude, go to the video store and rent any movie with a football storyline. At some point, in just about every one of these movies, when the team is about to lose the big game and the players need to be pumped up, the coach will belittle, anger, and presumably empower the team by calling them a bunch of girls. Why does that work? Because no insult could be worse!

But heterosexism, like sexism, is beginning to erode in society and in the church. For a very long time, most of the decisions affecting the world have been made by white, heterosexual, educated, Western men. Ever so gradually, though, people of color were invited to the conversation; then women; and now gay and lesbian people. And things are never the same when the oppressed claim — and receive — their voice. It's no wonder the resistance is so fierce, given that we're changing a system that's been in place almost forever.

But how do we move forward? And what is the rightful role of religion in this public discourse? Unlike some issues we've faced in the past, the movement forward in the civil realm is tied intimately to moving forward in the religious realm. There is perhaps no other prejudice, ensconced in the laws of the land, that's so based on sacred scripture, so entwined with our theological understanding of the nature of humankind and the sexuality that proves to be both its blessing and its curse. No other attitude in the body politic is so tied to an attitude stemming from a particular Judeo-Christian teaching. Change in no other social attitude in the secular culture is so tied to change in religious belief.

So it will take religious people and religious voices to undo the harm done by religious institutions. While there's been a decline in the number of people who experience and express their spirituality in and through formal religious institutions, religion is still a powerful force within the culture, and it generally works against progress in the inclusion and full civil rights for gay, lesbian, bisexual, and transgendered people. It's time that progressive Christians rescue the Bible from the Religious Right, which has held it hostage and claimed it as its own private territory for far too long. It's time that Christians and Jews actually read the holy scripture they claim as the basis of their beliefs, instead of simply believing what others tell them it says. It's time we use reputable scholarship, sound reason, and thoughtful exploration to understand what the words of scripture meant to the person who authored them and what they meant to the people for whom they were written, before deciding whether or not those words are binding on people outside that ancient cultural context. It's time that progressive religious people stop being ashamed of their faith and afraid to be identified with the Religious Right, and start preaching the good news of the liberating Christ to all God's children.

But what is a good, positive, and appropriate way to voice one's religious convictions in public discourse? I think it involves a simple shift in focus from the public to the private in these expressions. I'm free to express my own personal and religious reasons for coming to the opinions I express, but the minute I start arguing that you must come to those same opinions because my religious truth must be your truth too, then I violate the divide between private and public. Most alarming of all is when "my" truth becomes "the" truth, applicable to everyone. James Dobson and Pat Robertson are perfectly free to tell me about the religious beliefs that compel them to oppose the acceptance of gay people, but when they claim that their beliefs are right and true for all humankind, they move from democracy to theocracy.

Similarly, if I argue for the full inclusion of gay, lesbian, bisexual, and transgendered people in society, I must do so on the merits of my argument, not on a claim that my understanding of God is right and true and compelling for everyone. I must make my arguments based on decency, compassion, democratic principles, and a notion of the common good — not on any reading of any sacred text to which I might subscribe.

We need to separate, as best we can, the civil realm from the religious, especially in the struggle for equal civil marriage rights for all citizens. Clergy have long acted as agents of the state in the solemnization of marriages. Because a priest or rabbi or minister acts on behalf of the state in signing the marriage license and attesting to the proper enactment of the marriage, we've lost the distinction between what the state does and what the religious institution does. In fact, the state effects the marriage, while the church pronounces its blessing on it. In France, everyone is married at the mayor's office; those who are religious reconvene at the church for the religious blessing. Those who don't desire such a blessing are still fully married according to the laws of the state. In such an arrangement, it's clear where the state's action ends and the church's action begins.

We need to make a clear distinction between civil rights and religious rites. It may take many years for religious institutions to add their blessing to same-sex marriages, and no church or synagogue should be forced to do so, but that should not slow down progress toward the full civil right to marriage as executed by the state for the benefit and stability of the society. Because in New Hampshire civil unions became legal in January 2008, my partner of twenty years and I will enter into such a union. In a public building owned by the state, our legal, civil union will be solemnized by our female Jewish lawyer. That's the civil part, accountable to the state. Then we will walk down the street to St. Paul's Church for prayers of thanksgiving and blessing for our union — that is the purview of the church. Such a separation of the roles of church and state might be helpful in many ways. Perhaps it's a separation that ought to be made for all couples, heterosexual and homosexual alike.

In the end, I know this debate will turn out right. Christians are hopeful by nature — not because we have any special confidence in the desire of human beings to do the right thing, but because of our confidence in God to keep prodding, inspiring, and calling us until we do it. The world may be ready for change, but our faith tells us that change is anything but random. God is always working for the coming of the kind of kingdom in which all are respected, all are valued, all are included. I believe the Holy Spirit is working within the church and within the culture to bring that full inclusion about, and in the end, God will not be foiled. In the meantime, we need to work with all our might, intellect, dollars — and all our hearts — to bring that new world into existence.

✳ 3 ✳

SEX AND THE CITY OF GOD

Though I've been cast in the role of spokesman, icon, and rabble-rouser, mostly I think of myself as a simple country bishop and a human being in training. I spend a lot of my life trying to figure out how to be a good human. As a Christian, and as a bishop of the church, I've tried to understand my human-ness in relation to my creator, especially as revealed in Jesus Christ, as an avowed and practicing male. Every moment of my life has been filtered through that lens. I could no more know what it's like to have lived life as a woman than fly to the moon.

But one of the great rewards of being gay is that it's my little window into some of what it must be like to be a woman, or a person of color, or a person in a wheelchair — and countless other categories the dominant culture has controlled, diminished, and oppressed. Being male, being gay — those are two perspectives from which I've lived my life and understood sexuality.

Think for a moment about your own perspectives and the messages you received about sexuality while you were growing up. At best, most of us were confused about it; at worst, we were downright frightened — and fear is precisely the message we were meant to get. Not that sexuality is a wonderful gift from God, meant for our joy and pleasure and a means of communication with the beloved. But rather that sexuality is a horrifying Pandora's Box that must be kept sealed up, lest the demons of desire and passion come rushing out like so many uncontrollable banshees to devour our hearts and souls. My favorite of all these crazy-making messages is this: sex is dirty, save it for the one you love. Then, as tradition has it, in some magical and mysterious way, on our wedding night, sex is transformed into something wonderful and easy.

Now that I've raised two daughters I can see both sides of the picture. I love my daughters, and when they were teenagers I didn't want them to be hurt. I feared they'd make themselves vulnerable to deep and lasting pain by entering into sexual intimacy too soon and emotionally ill-equipped. And because the potential for hurt is so great in matters sexual, as a parent it's tempting to paint sexuality with a frightening brush, in hopes of scaring kids off. That's the motivation behind the "just-say-no" approach to both sex and drugs.

I've done a lot of AIDS education, especially with young people, and encountered a lot of folks who believe that "just say no" is all the AIDS education, and all the sex education, young people need. But this approach not only does little to protect our kids from AIDS, it teaches them the wrong things about sexuality. "Just say no" is offensive, condescending, and unhelpful. First of all, the word "just" makes it all seem so simple, as if any imbecile, certainly any Christian imbecile, would automatically know the right thing to do.

Saying no — and certainly saying no to intercourse outside marriage or a committed relationship — is a real option, even the safest, best option. But the word "just" robs this decision-making of its pain, confusion, and uncertainty. And that's true for teens as well as for twenty-, or thirty-, or forty-, or fifty-, or sixty-year-olds, and everyone in between and beyond.

Just say no to which part of sexuality? Say no to hugging, holding hands, to touching, to kissing, to massage? Say no to fondling? Say no to unbuttoning a blouse or shirt? Say no to fondling the breast or the chest? Say no to rubbing the legs, to unbuttoning the pants or skirt?

The real question isn't whether or not to be sexual; we are sexual every minute of our lives. The real question is what limits do we choose for our sexual activity, and by what criteria? We may need to say no to the most intimate expressions of sexual intimacy. But for the health of our bodies, and the health of our souls, we must *not* say no to sexuality — this marvelous means of communion that enlivens and blesses our daily existence.

Sex and Scripture

As Christians we must always and first turn to the biblical witness to explore the stories and the wisdom of the love affair between God and God's people to discern their perceptions of God's movement in their lives. And having understood their experience and their context, we must use our community's reason and experience to discern what the experiences written about in the Bible might mean for us.

But the Bible is much less clear and far less helpful about matters sexual than some would have us believe. Though we hear impassioned pleas for a return to biblical standards of sexuality, those standards aren't always clearly articulated, and there's much in the biblical practice of sexuality that no one would propose we emulate.

But first, the good news. The Hebrew scriptures offer a refreshing approach to sexuality — a lusty, earthy, and sensual telling of the human story as experienced by God's people. There's a kind of vulnerability in the early Hebrews, who are willing to describe themselves in all their imperfection, short-sightedness, and folly.

One thing is very clear from the Hebrew scriptures. Tim Sedgwick, professor of Christian ethics at Virginia Theological Seminary, points out that "scripture testifies that human sexuality stands at the heart of human identity."[1] The early Hebrews seemed to believe that sexuality is present, operative, and important to all we are and all we do as human beings. For them, it's never merely a matter of procreation, as it's been for much of

---

1. See the address by Dr. Timothy Sedgwick at Seabury-Western Theological Seminary, Evanston, Illinois, to the 1998 Provincial Synod of Province V.

Christendom. For the Hebrews, sex is also a grace-filled gift from God. It's no accident that in Hebrew, the verbs "to know" and "to create" both have as their source the verb that describes the genital, sexual act. It's a blessing to us and almost a miracle that the Old Testament canon includes the book known as the Song of Solomon — a series of poems that celebrate unashamedly the joys of human sexual love. Though this book has been interpreted and used devotionally to symbolize the desire for union between God and God's people, Israel — or by Christians to describe the relationship between Christ and his church — it still stands alone for its sheer delight in our human sexuality.

> How beautiful you are my love, how very beautiful! Your eyes are doves behind your veil...your lips are like a crimson thread, and your mouth is lovely. Your cheeks are like halves of a pomegranate behind your veil.... Your two breasts are like two fawns...eat, friends, drink, and be drunk with love. (4:1–5, 5:1b)

> And the beloved goes on to dream, "Listen! my beloved is knocking. Open to me, my sister, my love, my dove, my perfect one; for my head is wet with dew, my locks with the drops of the night.... My beloved thrust his hand into the opening, and my inmost being yearned for him.... I am faint with love." (5:2, 4, 8b)

The Song of Solomon is an ode to the sheer pleasure and joy of human sexuality, yet in our fear and our guilt, we've often lost that joy and delight to the proscriptions of "thou shalt not."

But other parts of the Old Testament are not a guide for healthy sexuality. We don't, for example, emulate the treatment of women in Old Testament times. We wouldn't advocate taking multiple wives or concubines; we wouldn't espouse treating women as property, nor understanding adultery as a crime committed by one man against the property of another. When we talk about the standards of biblical sexuality, let's think carefully about exactly what we mean.

The Bible expresses the values of the culture, time, and place in which it was written — values not necessarily binding on us. Counter to the claims of our conservative brothers and sisters, refusing to accept the culturally- and time-bound values related to women is not a rejection of the authority of scripture.

The epistles of the New Testament are more ambivalent about the joys of sexuality than the Song of Solomon. St. Paul uses marriage as the symbol of the mutually self-giving relationship of Christ to his church. Paul expected Jesus' second coming at any moment, and anything that took people's minds off preparing themselves for that event — including marriage and all matters sexual — was best avoided. Although St. Paul thought it was preferable to remain single, he bowed to the reality of human frailty and sin and admitted that if one had to have sex, they'd be better off married than aflame with passion and on the loose.

Paul and his Greek and Persian contemporaries were also influenced by a popular notion from which most of the Western world still operates — an idea that would have been foreign to the Hebrew mind and to Jesus — the notion of a mind/body dualism asserting that matters of the mind and soul were noble and striving for the good and perfect, while matters of the body were crude and obscene and inherently shallow, if not evil. And, of course, the noble strivings of the mind were always in danger of being undermined and destroyed by the gross desires of the flesh. Seeing the body, and especially sexuality, in this corrupting way is perhaps the most powerful source of our Pandora's-Box attitude toward sex.

But Jesus of Nazareth, whose life was permeated with earthiness and sensuality, stood much more in the tradition of the Song of Solomon than in the tradition of Pandora's Box. Women were central to his life and ministry; they traveled with him and even supported him financially. Even more remarkable is the unique —

and to the people of his day, scandalous — way he befriended
women, especially those condemned and scorned by society and
the religious establishment. He got into trouble for associating
with and standing up for adulterers and Samaritan women and
other questionable sinners. He always exhibited an infinite respect
for women, which was radically uncharacteristic of his time and
culture.

This isn't the picture of Jesus we learned in Sunday School,
probably because we've inherited the Greek mind/body dualism
and figure that Jesus had his mind on higher things. But Jesus
stands in the tradition that affirms the Old Testament notion
that sexuality is near the center of human identity, and that the
creation — including our physical bodies and our sexuality —
is good.

Ultimately, of course, for a look at a theology of sexuality,
we return to the story of the creation, as told in two different
versions in Genesis. In the first account, you can't help but notice
the recurring proclamation, "And God saw that it was good."
Humankind, created in God's own image, both male and female,
the pinnacle of the whole creation, is pronounced good.

But in the second account, Adam is created early on, formed
from the earth and then breathed into life by God. Only later
does God seem to realize that he's made a mistake. God notices
that Adam is lonely and in need of a helper and partner. And
this seems to be the justification for the creation not of woman
(at first), but of the animal kingdom — none of which satisfies
Adam's longing for a partner and helpmate.

But Adam gets to decide what fulfills him. God causes Adam
to fall asleep and fashions out of his rib a woman, whom Adam
immediately recognizes as his partner and helpmate. "This at last
is bone of my bones and flesh of my flesh; this one shall be called
Woman [*ishshah*], for out of Man [*ish*] this one was taken. . . . And
the man and his wife were both naked, and were not ashamed"
(Gen. 2:23–25).

Our faith community finds in these stories the creation of humankind that is good, that is made in the image of God, that is male and female, and that reflects the kind of unity and community intrinsic to the Godhead.

But consider how the second creation story has been used by Hebrews and by Christians, and by lots of other people down to our own time, to rationalize the subordination of women to men. It's clear to see how that understanding happened. After all, God seems to be saying, "Whoops, I knew I forgot something." And Eve seems to have been created only to fulfill Adam's need — clearly a subservient role.

To make matters more complicated, add one serpent and mix in a pinch of temptation. Women got a bad rap in Eden, and so have a lot of others who have been oppressed. This way of understanding scripture has even hurt men, who have been told to bear the entire burden and responsibility of creation without equal helpmates and partners. Men as well as women have paid a terrible price for this patriarchal arrangement.

Radical Vulnerability

But let's look at the creation stories a bit differently, by considering God in a new way — not just "immortal, invisible, God-only-wise," but God as intentionally and constitutionally vulnerable. It's only a small jump theologically to imagine that the loneliness Adam seems to have felt — his need for a companion — is reminiscent of the loneliness of Yahweh, who, while dwelling in the community of the Trinity, desired a creation to relate to. That shows us something important about the God who did the creating. Instead of fashioning puppets on a string, God, exhibiting the most extraordinary and unfathomable vulnerability, made us as creatures with free will who might or might not love God back. And ever since, God has been seeking us out as helpmates and partners in the world, longing for a relationship with us. The Old and New Testaments hardly speak of anything

else: from Jahweh longing for a closer and more faithful relationship with his people, to Christ pictured as the bridegroom of the
church, the Bible is the story of the longing of the lover for the
beloved. God stands at the door of our hearts, wanting in. God
becomes human in Jesus of Nazareth, intentionally making himself vulnerable yet again, to heal the brokenness between God's
self and God's creation.

Could it also be that God was revealing God's self in the very
act of creation? Our God-given freedom means God stands a
good chance of being disappointed by our inattention, if not our
outright rejection. Could it be that the capacity to be vulnerable is a large part of the image of God in which we're created?
The capacity to choose to be vulnerable, of course, is unnatu-
ral; it seems to fly in the face of the natural urge for survival.
But it gives us a third option to "fight or flight." As human
beings, created in the image of God, we can choose to make
ourselves vulnerable. Vulnerability is at the heart of the nature
of God.

Look at the last line of the second creation narrative: "And the
man and his wife were both naked, and were not ashamed" (Gen.
2:25). Nakedness, which most of us are taught to be ashamed
of, symbolizes the vulnerability with which Adam and Eve approached each other and God, with nothing to hide, nothing to
hold back from the beloved.

It wasn't long before people proved to be poor stewards of
others' vulnerability. First there was the mythic fall; with their dis-
obedience, Adam and Eve flung God's vulnerability in God's face.
And then, scripture says, "the eyes of both were opened, and they
knew that they were naked, and they sewed fig leaves together
and made loincloths for themselves" (Gen. 3:7). We've been violating one another's vulnerability ever since, feeling guilty and
trying to cover our nakedness. And we've been violating God's
vulnerability too.

Throughout the ages, God has tried to bridge that great chasm between us. Ultimately, God committed the supreme act of vulnerability, becoming human himself in the flesh of Jesus. Like the father of the prodigal son, God waits on the front porch, looking down the road for our return, hoping we'll come to our senses, repent of our wicked ways, and come home to the loving parental arms of God, where a feast of immense proportions awaits us. Can you just feel God's longing for a relationship? Can you feel how vulnerable God has made God's self? Can you feel how God's heart must be breaking?

The Vulnerability of Sex

Vulnerability has just about everything to do with sex; there's hardly a more vulnerable place to experience the joys and the dangers of vulnerability than in a sexual relationship. In few places is love of self and love of neighbor more important. When I do AIDS education and people ask me whether or not I believe in abstinence before or outside of marriage or a committed relationship, I say, "You bet I do." And that's because the chances are very good—human nature being what it is—that you, your sexual partner, or both, will get hurt along the way. We need to talk to kids and thirty-year old singles, and forty- and fifty-year old divorcees, about how vulnerable lovemaking makes you—not just to pregnancy and AIDS, but to damaged self-esteem, disappointment, and loneliness in the midst of the most physical, intimate connection two people can have. I'm far more worried for our children's sense of self-worth than I am about whether or not they are virgins on their wedding days, or the day they choose partners with whom to live out their lives. When I say I believe in abstinence that's what I mean.

The church affirms abstinence not because it was given as a commandment on Sinai, but because love of self and love of neighbor commend it. Lovemaking outside a committed, safe, protected, and protecting relationship is just plain risky, and sometimes dangerous. It's even risky *inside* a committed relationship.

Every time I make love I'm at risk. Right off the bat, I'm at risk because my partner may say no, and I must deal with rejection. And if my partner says yes, I begin to wonder: Will I feel good when this is over? Will I feel good about my body? Will I feel good about this person I'm with? Will I receive pleasure and warmth and the feeling of being loved? Will I be able to give those things? Will I be able to be present to this moment, and to this person? Will my partner be present to me? Will I have an orgasm, and will it matter? Will my partner have an orgasm, and will it matter? If the risks are this great with someone I love — if I am vulnerable in so many ways inside a committed relationship — then how much more at risk and vulnerable is a sixteen-year-old, or any of us, outside such a commitment?

The vulnerability inherent in God's creation of the world, and in God's becoming flesh in Jesus, is the key to unlocking the power and meaning of human sexuality. The spiritual and physical union between two people mirrors the relationship God desires with humankind. The longing of a husband for a wife, a lover for the beloved, mirrors God's longing for us. A lover's sheer delight in the body of the beloved reflects God's sheer delight in us.

When lovemaking is really right, it's perhaps as close as we can come to knowing the kind of desire and love God holds for us. When we fully give ourselves to another in lovemaking, we participate in the kind of self-giving love that God has for us. This kind of love is sacramental, offering a window into the heart of the Creator. When I can express with my body what I'm feeling with my heart, the integration of body and soul is astounding. That's what we mean when we say marriage signifies the mystery of the union between Christ and his church.

That kind of experience doesn't happen to us human beings very often, even in the context of marriage. It's an ideal that we're just too self-centered to manage very often. But if you've ever come close to it you know it. And you know you've participated in something more than great sex; it is a fleeting, momentary participation in the nature of God.

Making Sense of Sex

If vulnerability is at the heart of the nature of God, and if we can come close to God through the vulnerability we share in our intimate sexual relations, what can we say about those interactions? Are there standards by which we can judge our intimate sexual relationships? Or are conservatives right when they say we've tossed all sense of right and wrong to the wind?

I offer three criteria for judging the morality of sexual actions: equality, authenticity, and appropriate vulnerability. First, any healthy, wholesome, and moral sexual relationship requires an equality of the lovers. Partners need to be on the same footing for their sexual acts to be moral. We are all equal in the eyes of God. We are all of equal value, and no one side of the sexual relationship should be subordinate to the other.

Both partners in an intimate sexual relationship must enter that relationship as equals, free to lead and to follow, to say yes and to say no, to be bold and to be shy. Virtually every sexual problem brought to me as a priest — all the pain, discomfort, and dis-ease in the sexual relationships I've counseled both inside and outside marriage — has been related to inequality. Someone feels pushed too far, unable to say no; someone feels powerless in the face of the partner; someone feels the entire responsibility for the sexual relationship.

At its worst, of course, this inequality defines the abuse and sexual misconduct we hear so much about. At its root, child abuse is wrong because of the unequal power of any adult over any child. Sexual misconduct by clergy or professional counselors is wrong because it's an inappropriate and immoral use of the inherent inequality of the counselor/counselee relationship. Rape is by definition a circumstance of inequality, with one person exerting violent power over a less powerful victim. Incest is the manipulation of someone through fear of physical or emotional violence, or the fear of the loss of an important family relationship. The inequality of these settings defines the immorality.

While most of us aren't guilty of such gross immoralities and inequalities, let's not pat ourselves on the back. The overt and covert inequalities between men and women carry over into our relationships and marriages. Partnered gay and lesbian folks have a lot to teach heterosexuals in this regard. Much of the chaos in our society and in the church are the early stages of the end of male dominance, male superiority, and male privilege. And because of the link between homophobia and misogyny, this battle over homosexuality is as much about the end of patriarchy as anything else.

The Clarence Thomas–Anita Hill Supreme Court confirmation hearings were a watershed in male-female relations in the United States — not because we'll ever know who was telling the truth, but because Anita Hill described a relationship of inequality between males and females, which virtually every man and every woman in this country knows to be true. Working class or professional, educated or not, at some level American men know that the jig is up.

Second, we judge our relationships by their authenticity. In authentic sexual relationships, what we exhibit on the outside with our bodies reflects what's going on inside with our spirits. In a moral relationship of sexual intimacy, we connect our bodies and souls, refusing to separate the two. Men, it seems to me, are more apt to violate this standard than women, mostly because we're taught that separation from birth. It's okay, for instance, for boys to sow a few wild oats, sharpen their sexual skills on prostitutes or loose women, and carve as many notches in their bedposts as they can. Girls, on the other hand, are taught that love comes first and that lovemaking is an expression of that love.

We've seen more promiscuity among gay men, not because both men are gay, but because both men are men. Studies of lesbian women show little or no interest in promiscuity. Perhaps heterosexual men might be more promiscuous if the object of their affections weren't women who are less willing to participate in such casual encounters. So for relationships of such sexual intimacy to be moral and Christian, there must be an authentic expression of one's insides through the body, making that relationship sacramental.

Finally, a third criterion: Karen Lebacqz's notion of "appropriate vulnerability."[2] For a sexual relationship to be healthy and moral there must be a shared and equal vulnerability. Each partner must be a willing participant in the level of vulnerability chosen, un-manipulated and unthreatened. And to be proper, she maintains, the level of sexual expression should be commensurate with the level of commitment in the relationship. In other words, you don't have intercourse on the first date, even if you are equally vulnerable. Sexuality, a beautiful possibility, is also an easy place to get hurt. It's crazy and dangerous to make yourself so vulnerable to hurt in a relationship in which trustworthiness isn't present. There is serious vulnerability inside such a trusting relationship, never mind outside one.

Appropriate vulnerability is a criterion by which to question intimate sexual relationships between very young people, between casual acquaintances, or between anyone not in a relationship that includes a mutual commitment to love, honor, and trust the other, and to be trustworthy in return. Whatever the pitfalls and failures of marriage in practice, the commitment of a stable and monogamous marriage provides a supportive context for vulnerable expressions of the self. Marriage at its best ensures that the vulnerability of sexuality is a sacred trust to both partners, and

---

2. Karen Labacqz, "Appropriate Vulnerability: A Sexual Ethic for Singles," in *After the Revolution: The Church and Sexual Ethics*, series in the *Christian Century*, May 6, 1987.

that attempts at sexual intimacy remain protected in a mutually vulnerable and committed relationship.

Sex and the Book of Common Prayer

How does our tradition, as passed down through the ages, speak to these criteria? For us as Episcopalians, our tradition comes to us primarily through the prayer book, the closest thing we have to a systematic theology. If you want to know what we believe, look at how we pray. Check out the service for the celebration and blessing of a marriage: at the very beginning of the liturgy, we're given three purposes for which men and women seek to be united as husband and wife.

First, "the union of husband and wife in heart, body, and mind is intended by God for their mutual joy." That's as close as we come to asserting the delight, joy, and pleasure that can come in such a union.

Second, the prayer book tells us that marriage is for the help and comfort partners give one another in times of prosperity and adversity. It's a prayer for mutuality and for safety and for mutual nurture. It's the Genesis call for a helpmate and partner.

Lastly, the prayer book says that marriage is — when it is God's will — meant for the creation of children and their nurture in the knowledge and love of the Lord. This possibility of children is part of a larger purpose of marriage and union — generativity. There must be something about the relationship that results in the couple's seeing beyond themselves to caring about what happens with the world. Though having biological children is the most usual expression of generativity, it's not the only one. Generativity is the need and desire to find and be a part of things worth living and dying for, things to which we offer our selves, our time, and our money. That generative spirit will inspire us to invite neighbors in for dinner, serve as a godparent, adopt an orphan, coach a Little League team, and care what kind of environment we pass along to the next generation.

In a time of fanatic individualism, this mystical union of two people ought to be good for those beyond themselves — in the church, the community, and the world. This larger, communal purpose of marriage is evidenced in several of the liturgy's intercessory prayers for the couple. This view of marriage asks: "Will the world be a better place for having joined these two people together?" The blessing of their union is a thanksgiving to God for showing up in the relationship.

Just before the nuptial blessing we pray, "Make their life together a sign of Christ's love to this sinful and broken world, that unity may overcome estrangement, forgiveness heal guilt, and joy conquer despair. Give them such fulfillment of their mutual affection that they may reach out in love and concern for others." Our tradition passes along joy, mutuality, and generativity as the purposes and ends of Christian marriage, and within it sexuality.

The central doctrine of our Christian faith is the Incarnation, which we celebrate at Christmas. But Christmas is so prettied up with mangers and wise men and angels that we lose the wildly radical message of the Incarnation. The miracle of Christmas isn't the birth of a baby, but the reclaiming of human flesh, the declaration that humanity is an appropriate and honorable abode of almighty God. In the words of Richard Hooker, "God hath deified our nature, though not by turning it into himself, but by making it his own inseparable habitation."[3] As the opening of John's Gospel proclaims, "The Word became flesh and dwelt among us, full of grace and truth." That is good news that needs to be preached.

If we acted as if we truly believed the message of Incarnation, the world would be different. If we believed that human flesh was an appropriate and honorable abode for God and for ourselves; if we understood that our sexuality permeates all of who we are,

---

3. Quotation in the original English from the Folger Library Edition of the Works of Richard Hooker, vol. 2, *Of the Laws of Ecclesiastical Polity*, ed. W. Speed Hill (Cambridge, Mass.: Harvard University Press, 1977), V. 54.5.

and rejoiced in it; if we saw our souls and bodies as a reasonable, holy, and living sacrifice to God; if we pledged and found joy, mutuality, and generativity in our intimate sexual relationships, then people would be beating down the doors of our churches to find out what makes our lives so joyful, our relationships so full of mutual respect, and our outreach to the world so central to who we are. It's time we took off the fig leaves of guilt and ran around the Eden of our relationships with God, forgiven, naked, and free.

✳ 4 ✳

JUNE BRIDE

"I always wanted to be a June bride." As soon as the words were out of my mouth, I knew there'd be trouble. I'd just delivered an hour-long lecture on the relationship between religion and public discourse and why religious fervor over homosexuality plays such a large and negative role in the securing of full civil rights for gay people. During the question-and-answer period, someone asked me about the upcoming civil union between me and Mark, my partner of twenty years. The audience had been welcoming and sympathetic, full of laughter and understanding, and for one moment, I forgot that the C-SPAN cameras were rolling and that every word I said would be parsed by my critics.

Within hours, those eight words had made it around the world, thanks to conservative bloggers and the magic of the Internet. No context; nothing about the preceding hour of carefully constructed comments; nothing about my defense of — and love for — the scriptures; nothing about the loving God to whom I constantly pointed. Just this one sentence.

Surely no one thinks I'll don a wedding gown and wear flowers in my hair. But I suspect a lot of people are uncomfortable with me using the word "bride" — a word associated with women-as-property — to describe a man. For many centuries, marriage was about the transfer of property (the bride) from one man (the father) to another man (the groom) — in some places accompanied by the payment of a dowry or bride price. Is calling myself a "bride" offensive because it relegates a "privileged" man to the status of a woman? What could be worse than that! I'm not exactly sure why this statement has caused such an uproar, but I do know that the energy that pushed my statement around the world in no time flat has gone far beyond anything reasonable.

I regularly do media training to avoid this kind of faux pas. The media consultants impress on me that I will never again be in a "small room." Because of the high level of media attention, followed by the close scrutiny of those who oppose me, I'm never in a trusting, safe environment where I can let my guard down. Someone is always watching and will use anything I say against me. It's not paranoia if they really *are* out to get you.

I'll be the first to admit that it would have been better if I'd never uttered those eight words — not because they aren't true, but simply because they gave the conservative forces something else to use against me. It was a stupid thing to say, and I should have known better.

What I should have said was something like this: "Gay and lesbian people grow up with the same hopes that other people do — that they'll be able to celebrate their love for one another with family and friends gathered around, pledging their support for the faithful, monogamous, life-long intentioned, holy vows they've just taken. I too have always longed for such a day." Instead, I simply said, "I've always wanted to be a June bride." And all hell broke loose.

The worst part is that it's reminiscent of the years and years that I had to self-censor everything I said, so as not to give away the fact that I was gay. Gay and lesbian people learn at an early age to filter every single word before uttering it, straining out anything that might indicate who we really are on the inside. I know from my own experience and from countless others that this is an exercise in self-alienation. In a nanosecond, we listen in our heads to what we're about to say and, before speaking, edit out anything that might indicate to the listener that we're gay. We get really, really good at it, until it becomes second nature. But it takes a toll on our souls.

This may not sound like oppression — it's not the same as being thrown into prison or burned at the stake — but it's one of the silent, painful results of oppression. The result of any oppression is living in fear — fear of discovery, rejection, and retribution. It's what most gay and lesbian people live with every day, all over the world.

A fellow bishop, responding to my "June bride" comment, recently questioned the appropriateness of my having a civil union just before the once-a-decade Lambeth Conference of the bishops of the Anglican Communion. He suggested that to spare the Communion further distress, Mark and I should cancel our plans. Though admitting to not knowing (or presumably, caring about) the context in which I spoke, or even knowing whether the report was accurate, the bishop criticized my words all the same.

Why a civil union? Why take advantage of the new civil law permitting such a social arrangement, provided for by the state of New Hampshire to support the stability and societal good that comes from having committed, faithful gay families in the state? It seems too obvious a question to need an answer, but apparently not so.

Mark and I have been together for twenty years. In much the same way that women have done for countless generations, Mark left a great career with the Peace Corps to make a life with me and my daughters in New Hampshire. I'd made it clear right from the beginning that I'd never leave them. For all that time, we've shared our lives in every aspect. Although a fiercely private person, Mark wholeheartedly supported me in responding to God's call to the episcopate, and when my election took place, and ever since, he's stood by my side — in the uncomfortable limelight — as my partner and spouse.

We've dealt with all the ramifications of being a gay couple in our culture. All the protections that exist for heterosexual couples were not automatically available to us. At considerable cost, we legally contracted some of these: durable power of attorney for financial and medical decisions, inheritance (of course, an inheritance tax would be imposed on him as if he and I were complete strangers), a trust for him and our children. But literally hundreds of rights and protections afforded heterosexual couples at the utterance of "I do" are not available to us. The kind of protections that became instantly available to Britney Spears — who, on a lark, decided one night in Las Vegas to get married — are not available to Mark and me despite twenty years of love and fidelity.

Imagine for a moment that you've been in a same-sex relationship. When you and your partner return from overseas on a plane and the flight attendants distribute customs and immigrations forms — "one per family" — you and your partner will need two forms because your family is *not* a family, though you've been together many years. When you seek coverage under your partner's medical insurance plan, your partner will have to pay income taxes on this benefit, unlike your heterosexual colleague in the next cubicle. When your partner is unconscious after an auto accident, you will have to contact her next-of-kin to make medical decisions, because you are nobody. In the eyes of the state, you have *no* relationship. When your partner dies, you have to hope for good relations with your partner's parents, because they have legal charge over her body and its burial while you, in contrast, have no rights at all.

Now that some — though not even half — of these rights and protections have been afforded by an act of the New Hampshire legislature, why would we not take advantage of them? If loving one's spouse should come at the top of the list of one's priorities and commitments, how or why would I say to Mark, "We really shouldn't do this because some people in the Anglican Communion will be upset"? Our union will not be marriage, with the more than one thousand federal and state rights that instantly accrue to a traditional married couple. But it will offer us something. Does Mark not deserve — do *we* not deserve — the protections now available to us?

Early on, the press erroneously reported that Mark and I had planned to have a civil union one minute after midnight on New Year's morning. I was accused of trying to draw attention to myself by being the first in New Hampshire to take advantage of the new law — "media-mongering," they called it. The *Times* of London reported that we would be "married" on July 4 and "honeymoon" at Lambeth. Now I'm being accused of intentionally poking a finger in Lambeth's eye by scheduling the service in June. But if we'd waited until after Lambeth to announce our intentions, I'd be just as severely criticized for having been disingenuous and secretive about the civil union in order to assure an invitation to Lambeth. There is *no* time when our civil union will be acceptable to many in the Anglican Communion. But I will not be irresponsible to the partner and love of my life just to avoid giving offense.

Why not just a civil ceremony? Why a blessing too? When I testified before legislative committees for legal civil unions in New Hampshire, I argued for separating the civil *right* of unions from the religious *rite* of blessing. Mark and I will solemnize our union in a building owned by the state, signifying the civil authority for this union, and then proceed across the street to St. Paul's Church, where we will give thanks for our union and ask God's — and the gathered community's — blessing on us. We contemplated participating in a simple Eucharist, without any words of blessing, out of deference to the Anglican Communion. But does anyone think that the headlines would have read: "Gay bishop carefully steers clear of offending Communion"? No matter what we do, no matter what we say, our union will be pitched as an intentional affront to the Communion, and there isn't a single thing I can do about that. And because the blessing of unions has gone on in the Diocese of New Hampshire since 1996 (seven years before my election), why should the bishop not be entitled to the same pastoral care offered to other people in the diocese?

But why not just make it a "private" service — a solution offered by some in the Anglican Communion? But "private blessing" is an oxymoron. Although our service will be by invitation only, and out of sight of the press, our understanding of marriage is that the couple makes their vows public, in the presence of the gathered community, seeking the community's prayers and assistance in being faithful to those vows. By its very nature, marriage is a public event. Much as we have discontinued "private" baptisms in the back of the church on a Sunday afternoon in favor of the public incorporation of the newly baptized into the gathered community at Sunday-morning worship, so the blessing of unions, like marriage, is a public, communal event. To relegate it to a private, secretive venue is to violate its very nature.

When I was growing up, I could never have imagined same-sex couples being "out," never mind being married or partners in a civil union. There were no role models for a happy, productive life as a gay or lesbian person — no Billie Jean King or Greg Louganis, no Ellen DeGeneres, no Ambassador James Hormel, no Congressman Barney Frank. We had not yet been told that Walt Whitman, Tennessee Williams, and W. H. Auden were all gay; nor did we know that it was a renowned pacifist, Bayard Rustin, who happened to be gay, who taught Martin Luther King Jr. about nonviolent resistance. My life might have been very different had I known these things.

Our civil union will no doubt be reported by the press. I can't stop that. But I can rejoice that somewhere in Idaho or Ontario or Sussex, there's a gay boy or a lesbian girl who will read about it and know that they too can aspire to a healthy, whole life with a person of the same sex — and that they don't have to give up their faith along the way. It might occur to them that they too can put their sexuality and their spirituality together in a way that makes for happiness and spiritual depth. Like me, they may have "always dreamed of being a June bride." But unlike me, they will know it is possible.

Part Two

FAITH AND LIFE

Everyday Christianity

Almighty and eternal God, so draw our hearts to you, so guide our minds, so fill our imaginations, so control our wills, that we may be wholly yours, utterly dedicated to you; and then use us, we pray you, as you will, and always to your glory and the welfare of your people; through our Lord and Savior Jesus Christ. Amen.

— Prayer of Self-Dedication,
The Book of Common Prayer, pages 832–33

FOLLOWING JESUS CHRIST is a personal decision with communal consequences. We cannot be Christian alone, but we must go to God, alone and often, if we are to communicate with the One who enlivens, guides, and sustains us. Submission to God is a nearly universal theme ("Islam" means submission), but unless we get to know the God to whom we submit, it is a hopeless task.

We cannot preach the good news about a God we do not know. God stands at the doorway of our hearts but will not barge in uninvited. Our spiritual lives provide the space to invite God in, to know God directly, to allow our wills to be shaped by God's will, and to return to the world ready to serve in God's Name.

* 5 *

I *LOVE* THE BIBLE

I *love* the Bible. With no reservation, no holding back.

I grew up in a Bible-believing congregation of the Disciples of Christ Church. Every Sunday morning, from ten till eleven, every member of the church, young and old, went to Sunday School, and the study was always and only about scripture. From eleven till twelve, we worshiped God, always from the perspective of scripture. We were steeped in the sacred Jewish and Christian texts, and we believed that compliance with their teachings was the key to understanding God, discerning God's will for us, and claiming the salvation won for us on the cross.

Ours was a small congregation, without the resources to employ a full-time minister. So our minister was always — and continues to be — a seminarian from the College of the Bible (now Lexington Theological Seminary). My parents and the elders of this little church read the scriptures every day and taught me the value of doing so. Scripture guided everything we did.

But the experience I had as a child and as a teenager that sealed my love for the Bible was this — and I consider it a miracle, a theophany: I heard God's voice coming through those scriptures. I'd already begun to wonder about my "difference," the fact that I wasn't like other boys, and the thought scared me to death. My church was using the words of scripture to say that people who were attracted to others of the same sex were despicable, an "abomination," in the eyes of God. And yet — and here's the miracle — I heard God saying to me the words God said to Jesus at his baptism: "You are my Son, the Beloved; with you I am well pleased" (Luke 3:22). It may not make any sense to anyone reading these words, but I swear to you that despite what my church was teaching, I heard God's voice in scripture saying to me — to *me!* — "You are my beloved." And it saved my life.

Over the last thirty-five years, I have professed at each of my three ordinations: "I solemnly declare that I do believe the holy scriptures of the Old and New Testaments to be the Word of God, and to contain all things necessary to salvation." I made that declaration without hesitation, without any internal "buts," without crossing my fingers behind my back. I still declare it, with all my heart.

But what do I mean when I say it? What does the Episcopal Church — indeed the Anglican tradition — mean when it professes such a belief? Since our current divisions are purportedly about scripture and its authority over us, perhaps it's time to go a bit deeper.

I've often heard it said that the Bible is the story of the love affair between God and God's people. Taken as a whole, the Bible paints a picture of God in God's unrelenting attempts to get through to us. The Hebrew scriptures show God's unending patience, always offering unfaithful people another chance, always calling them back to faithfulness despite their journeying far from God. Perhaps God called Jews to be the "chosen" because of their willingness to describe themselves in all their unfaithfulness, in all their sinfulness, with honesty and candor. The Christian scriptures show us how far God was willing to go to reveal God's self, miraculously choosing to become one of us, showing us the true nature of God and calling us back through Jesus' sacrifice on the cross.

But how should we understand these sacred texts? In what way are they "holy"? How do we know what authority they should have over our lives? Were they inspired by God? Are their words inerrant? Was God's revelation of God's self complete when the canon of scripture was closed?

First, let's remember that the real, actual "Word" of God is Jesus, the Christ. As the Gospel of John so beautifully begins, "In the beginning was the Word. And the Word was with God, and the Word was God." That "Word" proceeding from the mouth of God, and existing concurrently with God since before time, is the Second Person of the Trinity, Jesus Christ. Jesus himself was the only perfect revelation of God.

All too often we forget that the holy scriptures, while the Word of God, are not the *words* of God, dictated from on high by a heavenly author. The words of scripture are a snapshot — a kind of time-lapse photo spanning fifteen hundred years of human-kind's encounter with the Living God. The authors of the many books of the Bible are witnesses to the action of God in their own lives.

The Hebrew scriptures contain many of our most beloved stories of God's interaction with God's people and describe the movement of God in calling them to do things on God's behalf — from building an ark to sacrificing a son, from calling cities to re-pent and reform their treatment of the poor to calling a shepherd boy to be king and his son to build a temple in Jerusalem. The Gospels give us three accounts of the life of Jesus, in the Synoptic Gospels of Matthew, Mark, and Luke, plus one theological reflec-tion in the lyrical and beautiful Gospel of John on the meaning of those events and that holy life. Mark's, the earliest of these accounts, was written some three decades after Jesus' death and resurrection; John's, the last, over a half-century after his ascen-sion. As four witnesses to an accident might each notice different aspects and describe the event in different ways, each of the Gos-pel writers offers a different perspective, from a particular point of view and with a particular audience in mind.

The rest of the New Testament contains the stories of how the community surrounding Jesus came to believe that he was still alive, still guiding them, still calling them into "the Way." Letters to the earliest communities of believers reveal that there was almost always conflict and disagreement among those who followed "the Way," and many of the letters of St. Paul urged these infant "churches" to live up to the way of life espoused by the earthly Jesus and live into the resurrected life he promised.

The Bible is a collection of many accounts of what it's like to encounter the Living God. They are dramatic stories about what happens when God cares enough about creation to be actively engaged in it. They are faithful accounts of the indescribable; they are words used to recount that for which there are no words: the mystery of God.

Are those words holy? Absolutely. Are they inspired? I believe they are. But are they inerrant? I don't believe so. Because the people who authored those accounts were not inerrant. They were faithful people describing — and testifying to — the meaning of God's actions in their lives.

That is "all" the Bible is. Though it's not inerrant, it's *not* unimportant, mistaken, or worthy of dismissal. It's a compelling, useful, and *primary* source of our knowledge of how God works in the lives of human beings to bring them abundant life and everlasting salvation. That is no small thing. For countless generations it has been the foundations of our faith and a witness to God's love that commands our love and respect.

Perhaps this brings us to a deeper understanding of the Anglican tradition's "three-legged stool" of authority — scripture, tradition, and reason. Scripture is always named first, as it should be, since it is our oldest, most cherished, and most authoritative account of God's love for us. But what of "tradition" and "reason?"

If scripture is a collection of the accounts of people of faith about the working of God in their lives, then "tradition" is the history of how the church has come to understand, interpret, and use those testimonies in the life of the church and the lives of the faithful. Over the last two thousand years, Christians have struggled with what those stories and events meant, and what continuing authority they have over contemporary lives.

Is "tradition" inerrant? Of course not. Like those who authored the various parts of the Bible, those Christians who have come after are not inerrant either. Their lives are not perfect, nor are their interpretations of scripture, nor are the decisions they made because of those understandings. We don't have to look far to find evidence: the Crusades and the Inquisition are obvious examples of how misguided we followers of Christ can be when it comes to putting biblical values into action. But beyond those obvious examples, can we also not see how far the "tradition" has strayed from the revelation of God in Christ? Could the church's "jumping into bed with Power" during the reign of Constantine really have been something Jesus imagined or hoped for? Could the church's accumulation of unimaginable wealth, which continues to this day, have been what Jesus longed for when he cautioned against the corrosive power of possessions? Could the disregard and ill-treatment of the poor, so condemned in both the Hebrew and Christian scriptures, be the sort of thing Jesus had in mind?

Still, the "tradition" is important for several reasons. First of all, we're too ready to assume that we know more than anyone else, that our own thoughts and experience trump all that's gone before. So the tradition is a check on our all-too-easy self-confidence. We need to learn and understand what our forebears have thought about God and about God's will for us before charging ahead to do our own thing. The history of the church, though it has its share of regrettable actions, is also replete with holy and courageous people of staggering faith, people who risked life and limb to be the loving arms of God in the world. Countless people of faith have written theology, poetry, prayers, and reflections that dwarf our own meager attempts at spirituality and are worthy of our study and thoughtful consideration. There is much in the tradition that, while not inerrant, is to be commended to modern-day Christians as worthy of our careful and prayerful attention.

Today, in the midst of a struggle between those who suggest that we change the "tradition" of a particular understanding of scripture and those who resist such a revision, it's instructive to note how many times within our two-thousand-year tradition — always with confusion and pain — the church has changed its understandings. Just a couple of examples:

Marriage, for most of the first millennium, was seen as a legal arrangement, blessed by the church, to provide for the proper, peaceful, and orderly transfer of property: of the woman (or sometimes, young girl) from one man, the father, to another, the husband; and of land and property to those who deserved them by virtue of marriage and legitimacy. Since such concerns were relevant only to those who owned any property to be transferred, marriage was regarded as unnecessary for ordinary people. That changed in the Middle Ages, and a fuller understanding of the sacrament of Holy Matrimony developed; today marriage is understood as a sacrament open to and commended to all heterosexuals. And the notion of marriage-for-love is a concept that appeared only in modern times.

Slavery, commonplace in the narratives of both the Hebrew and Christian scriptures, continued to exist into the nineteenth century, when abolitionists began to argue against it. Both sides in that debate quoted scripture to bolster their arguments. In the end, slavery was abolished (though it is not unheard of today), and the church changed its position on the institution of slavery, which it had held for nearly nineteen hundred years.

Much closer to our own time are two major changes in the church's understanding of its structure and its pastoral ministry. For nearly two thousand years, the church accepted St. Paul's notion that it was inappropriate for women to assume leadership positions in the life of the church (though elsewhere Paul writes that in Christ "there is neither male nor female"). Put crudely, tradition held that it was the lot of women to keep their heads covered and their mouths shut in church. Then, following several other Protestant churches, the Episcopal Church changed its mind and its canons to permit the ordination of women in 1976. In 1989, Barbara Harris became the first woman bishop in the entire Anglican Communion, though her orders, and those of countless other women deacons, priests, and bishops, are still not accepted by many in the Anglican Communion.

At roughly the same time, another dramatic change occurred that not only flew in the face of tradition, but seemed to disregard words that came from the mouth of Jesus himself. For countless centuries, anyone divorced and then remarried was unwelcome at Communion; subsequent marriages could not be presided over or blessed by Episcopal clergy. Indeed, for nearly two thousand years, the church understood Jesus' words to be literally true — that such marriages were adulterous and beyond the blessing or affirmation of the church.

But the church began to realize that we were denying Communion to members when they were most in need of it, and we saw with our own eyes that these second marriages were a blessing not only to the couple, but to the community of which they were a part. Over time, we began to ask, "Might our understanding of what God wants be too severe, too unpastoral, too unresponsive to God's less-than-perfect children?" Over time — and, it should be noted, accompanied by controversy — the Episcopal Church changed its mind. Now the solace and sustenance of Holy Communion is offered to those who have been divorced, and with appropriate counseling and with permission of the bishop, subsequent marriages may be solemnized and blessed in the church. A very long tradition was changed.

This leads us to the much larger question: Did God complete self-revelation in holy scripture, or does God continue to reveal God's self, throughout history and even today?

There's a much-neglected and seldom-quoted passage of scripture in John's Gospel that reports Jesus' words to his disciples on the night before he died: "I still have many things to say to you, but you cannot bear them now. When the Spirit of truth comes, he will guide you into all the truth" (John 16:12–13a). Jesus is saying, "You are not ready to hear everything I have to teach you — things you cannot culturally comprehend right now. So I will send the Holy Spirit to guide you and teach you, over time, those things which you need to understand."

The changes we've seen in our understanding of scripture over the nineteen centuries since it was written have happened through the guidance of the Holy Spirit. God hasn't changed God's mind, but our ability to apprehend and comprehend the mind of God is limited and sometimes faulty. Things that seemed simply "the way of the world" — like slavery, polygamy, and the lower status of women — in retrospect seem like examples of humankind's flawed, limited, and mistaken understanding of God's will. Our ability to better discern God's will has improved with time, prayer, and reflection.

This is good news for Christians. God didn't stop revealing God's self with the closing of the canon of scripture. God is still actively engaged in ongoing revelation over time, even in our own day. God didn't just "inspire" the scriptures to be written and then walk away, wishing us well in our attempts to understand those words. God's Holy Spirit continues to lead us into all the truth, as Jesus promised on the night before he was betrayed.

This gives us a whole new way to understand our beloved Anglican Communion's three-legged stool of authority. *Scripture* is the inspired accounts of encounters with the divine, written by people who knew the Jahweh of the Hebrew scriptures and the Christ of the Christian scriptures, and set down, in the best words they could conjure, what they learned about God in these encounters. *Tradition* is the two-thousand-year history of the church as Christians have grappled with those scriptural accounts, seeking to understand them and apply them in their own lives — and changing former understandings through their own encounters with the Living God through the Holy Spirit.

Finally, *reason* is the authority that presents itself in our own lives. We not only experience life in our own day and time, but we experience God in the midst of our lives, through the power of the Holy Spirit, who continues to lead us into truth. Sometimes that leading prompts us to change understandings we may have held for centuries. The good news in all this is that we worship a God who isn't locked up in scripture, but a God who is alive and well and active in our midst, continuing to lead us forward in our understanding of God's unchanging truth.

To learn about God, we always begin with scripture, which, after the full and perfect revelation of the Word, Jesus the Christ, is our primary source. Then we look at how the church has understood those words of scripture over time. And then we use our own experience and reason to ask what all this might mean for us today. Because we are always prone to shaping everything, including God's will, to our own ends, we must be careful as we apply "reason" in this triad of authorities. No one person can decide that our former understandings are faulty; changes that veer from long-held understandings must always be made in community. Many minds and hearts, working prayerfully together, must be employed in this delicate discernment of God's will. But this is a task we must not neglect, for to do so is to reject the leading of the Holy Spirit that has been promised to us.

The current debate in the Anglican Communion over sexuality is a contemporary example of the Holy Spirit leading us toward a fuller grasp of God's truth. Does that seem like a self-serving idea? Only time will tell. The process of discerning God's will never ends. It takes all of us — those who seek a change and those who resist it. And it takes courage even to ask if we might have gotten it wrong in the past. But this is what we're asked to do by the Living God, who promised to send the Holy Spirit to guide us into all truth, who promised to teach us the things we couldn't bear in an earlier time.

I *love* the Bible. I owe my faith and my life to the Bible and to its liberating message. It is in the Bible that I first met Jesus, and because of that, when I see Jesus acting in my own life, I recognize him. Scripture was the source of my belief that God loved me. Scripture was the source of my faith that — like the lepers and prostitutes and tax collectors and other outcasts — I too am included in God's embrace. I steep myself in the Bible's words and stories; I am refreshed, challenged, indicted, and liberated by its sacred words. Scripture reminds me of who I am and how God longs for a relationship with me. It assures me that no matter how often or for how long I may forget God, God never forgets or abandons me.

Where would I be — where would any person of faith be — without the Bible?

* 6 *

DAILY RESURRECTION

You can call the resurrection a doctrine of faith, and every Sunday when you recite the creed, you can tell the world you believe in it. But for me, and probably for you too, it goes way deeper.

I believe in resurrection because I have experienced it. Encountering a stone in my life that I could not remove on my own, surrendering to a God whose power can move stones — and mountains — and then receiving the life God wants for me *is* resurrection.

A couple of years ago, I took part in a treatment program for alcoholism and emerged into a new life of sobriety. During treatment I was told that abstaining from alcohol was the easy part. The hard part, the experts said, was learning to live a truly sober and conscious life, grateful to the God who makes it possible. As the years go by, I'm coming to understand that the "sober life" has to do with a daily surrender to God working in my life, doing for me things I cannot do for myself. The sober life is learning to work in partnership with God to live the abundant life Jesus promised would be mine in God's reign.

Easy enough to say. Pretty tough to do. Every single day, one day at a time, I have to do as those women did on that cold Easter morning: look up, and see, and believe that the stone has already been rolled back.

Those women approached the tomb to complete a proper burial for their friend and would-be messiah. Dread and sorrow filled their hearts, but like women everywhere, in every time, they came simply to do what had to be done. Jesus, who'd made the lame walk, and proclaimed the forgiveness of sins, and talked of a new life under the reign of God, was dead. For these women, the tomb, sealed with an enormous stone, was the end of a dream — their dream of salvation and deliverance.

But when they got to that tomb and looked up, they saw that the stone had already been rolled back.

They saw what had happened, but they could scarcely comprehend it. The stone that covered the tomb — the stone that weighed so heavily on their broken hearts — was gone.

It's like that for us, too. I know it's been like that for me. The stones that get in the way of our living a resurrected life are so large, so intimidating, so seemingly final, so frightening, that we keep our heads down, assuming they're simply unmovable. But every now and then, we're invited — even compelled — to look up, just as those women did that morning, and notice that that stone has already been rolled back.

You'd think I wouldn't need reminding. Years ago, my sexuality seemed like an immovable stone in my way, a burden so huge that it seemed to threaten everything I held dear. Accepting the fact that I was gay was impossible enough; affirming and embracing it was beyond comprehension. And then just as surely as Jesus called to his friend Lazarus to "Come out!" of his tomb, Jesus called me to come out of my tomb of guilt and shame, to accept and love that part of me that he *already* accepted and loved. If I would only look up and see that the stone had already been rolled away, I could have a new, more abundant life. That resurrection changed my life. I thought I would never, ever forget.

But I'm human. I forget from time to time that God has accomplished the most amazing thing in the life, death, and resurrection of Jesus Christ — something cosmic and yet entirely personal and individual. And God is always calling me back when I encounter stones in my way, reminding me to stop, look up, and see that the stone has already been rolled away, if I will only see it, surrender to it, and be changed and empowered by it.

Stones can come in many sizes and shapes, but what all these "stones" have in common is the ability to obscure what "life on the other side" of the stone is like. When somebody's thinking about leaving an abusive or destructive marriage, it's hard to imagine life on the other side of divorce. When somebody's addicted, it's virtually impossible to imagine life without the drug of choice. When some thorny issue needs to be dealt with in a relationship, the anxiety about what will result from honest confrontation may seem like too big a risk to take.

Or more positively, a person may feel a call to ordination, but there seems to be no way to pursue the call, given the time, resources, and spiritual demands it entails. Someone may feel called to a deeper relationship, but fear of the intimacy and commitment that requires may seem like a huge stone in the road. Any possibility of new life always involves the grief and loss of leaving an old life. Even if the old life is painful, at least it's familiar. It's always tough to roll that stone away. No wonder the women went away from the empty tomb afraid on that cold morning. The other disciples were afraid too, by all accounts. What if it were true that Jesus was alive, that God had rolled away the stone in their path to the resurrected life? Their lives would never be the same. And they weren't. And neither will our lives be.

Surrendering to the truth and power of the resurrection means embracing the knowledge that there is no good excuse anymore for letting those stones get in the way. The stone has been rolled back, and now the hard work of living a resurrected life begins, for each of us. Living our lives in that truth means doing courageous and mighty things in Jesus' name. Surrendering to the resurrection means letting go of all the anxiety and fear that can so easily grip us and leave us powerless, and experiencing the joy of the resurrected life. It means living our lives with "the peace that passes all understanding" in our hearts. And it means stopping each and every day, one day at a time, to look up and be reminded that the stone has already been rolled away.

✳ 7 ✳

FEAR NOT

We hear a lot about "homeland security" these days. Did you know that in the month following the tragic events of September 11, 2001, gun sales in the United States jumped 22 percent, and that now there's a handgun or shotgun for every man, woman, and child in America? Is there any doubt that "security" issues, at home and abroad, "drove" recent elections in the United States and elsewhere? Our anxiety about security is so acute, it now comes color-coded. An "orange alert" tells us to be more anxious about our safety, without giving us a place or time or method to avoid the danger — just be more anxious! Some of us are afraid to fly; some are afraid to invest; some are afraid to go overseas; some are nervous about opening their mail. Some of us are afraid of what we might have to learn about ourselves as a community of nations if we honestly ask why some people in the world hate us so much. Some of us fear losing our jobs; many are afraid to be generous in their giving, fearing what the future might hold. Some of us are fearful because we find ourselves in a shaky marriage; some are fearful because of the uncertainty and pain of a recent divorce; some of us fear intimacy with another; some of us fear being alone. Some of us fear the pain and change of confronting an addiction — in ourselves or someone close to us. Some of us face a life-threatening illness in ourselves or our families. There are so many things to be fearful of on any given day.

And yet, time and again, God's message to us is "fear not." God sent a whole slew of angels to ordinary humans proclaiming those very words in the midst of the most fearful circumstances. To Mary, a first-century Palestinian peasant girl about to have an out-of-wedlock child. To shepherds, tending their sheep, minding their own business, when the Angel Tabernacle Choir shows up on the hillside. To Joseph, the decent and kind man whose fiancée has somehow gotten herself pregnant and made *him* the butt of every joke in Nazareth. To a trio of Eastern astrologers who take a different route home because Herod is killing every child in Palestine under the age of two. (Terrorism is not new; the slaughter of innocents has been going on for a long, long time.)

All those angels seem to be hopelessly naive and just don't understand the ways of the world. Or maybe something else is going on. What in God's Name could take the fear out of these fearful situations? What was happening in Nazareth, or Bethlehem, or wherever these angels decided to show up, that could possibly make the exhortation to "fear not" remotely possible? And what could those exhortations possibly have to do with you and me, sitting in Manchester, New Hampshire, or Manchester, England, or Kuala Lumpur or Kigali, two thousand years later?

Stories with angels are usually very pretty, or so you'd think if you went by the greeting card companies and the purveyors of religious knick-knacks. But the angels are really harbingers of a dirty and tough story. After all, God was doing a *dirty* thing. No deity in the ancient world worth his salt would want to become human. Gods, after all, dwell in the heavens, untainted by the lowliness of humankind. Fine for humans to strive to become god-like. But God, desiring to become human? I don't think so.

But that's the foundation of our faith — not so much angels and babies and stars, but the Incarnation. The "c-a-r-n" of incarnation is the same root word we hear in "chili con carne" — which is chili with *meat*. The Incarnation is God's decision to put meat on God's self. To become enfleshed. For so long, humankind had wandered in darkness, making crude guesses about what God was really like. And if you read much of the Old Testament, you see that people like Abraham, Moses, and King David didn't always get it right. But because God loved us so much, and so wanted a relationship with us, God did the only thing God knew to do: God became one of us to get to know us from the inside, to walk with us and understand us, with all our hopes and fears and heartbreaks and joys. He didn't show up in a nice house, laid in a baby blue bassinet. He was born on the edges of society, into a despised race, in a conquered and occupied nation, to lowly, uneducated, scared-to-death teenaged parents, in a feeding trough — no more than a hole dug out of the floor of the cave out back, in which animals were locked up for safekeeping. God becomes a little baby, nursing at his mother's breast, while Joseph waves his hand over them both, trying to keep the flies away. The incarnation is dirty business because this humanity of ours, especially for those who live at the edges, is messy and not always pretty. Yet because of God's love for us and God's longing for intimacy with us, God wanted to be a part of it.

God wasn't doing only this dirty thing — becoming human — but also a tough thing. In a mystery too miraculous to comprehend, God decided not to merely *pretend* to be human, but actually to *become* fully human — giving up all divine prerogatives, astoundingly limiting God's self to the experiences of one human being, living in the world of Roman-occupied Palestine. The Incarnation was a tough love that finds its end in the intimacy and heartbreaking sorrow of the Last Supper, in the desperate plea in the Garden of Gethsemane to make it all go away, in the humiliation and degradation of Jesus' arrest and trial, and finally, on Good Friday, in his death on a criminal's cross, deserted by nearly all his friends and family — even seemingly deserted by God.

And all because God loves us just that much. To become human, "to live and die as one of us, to reconcile us to [Him], the God and Father of all" (BCP, p. 362). Now, there will be no more guessing, no more doubt about what God is like — because God has laid all God's cards on the table. We only have to look at this man Jesus to know just how loving and forgiving our God is. God *is* the loving father, ready to welcome back his prodigal sons and daughters — not waiting for our apologies but running to meet us and celebrate our homecoming. And in raising Jesus from the dead, God tells us that even in death there will be no end to our relationship with God.

And of course the real blessing of the Incarnation is that our relationship with God starts any time we're ready. And we can *have* a relationship with God because God knows us. God has been one of us. We worship a God who's literally "been here, done that." And it makes all the difference.

In an episode of the TV show *The West Wing,* Leo McGarry, the president's chief of staff, tells a story to his assistant, who's having a really hard time. Leo promises to be there for his friend and reminds him that he knows about hard times, because he himself is a recovering addict. He tells his story with a kind of twelve-step authority and wisdom:

It seems that there was a guy walking along an unfamiliar road, and he falls into a huge hole, with steep, vertical sides well above his head. He calls out for help. A doctor comes by, writes out a prescription and tosses it in the hole. Not much help there. Then a priest happens by and, in response to the call for help, kneels down, says a prayer, and goes on his way. Finally, another man comes along, and hearing the cry for help, promptly jumps into the hole. The first man says, "Are you stupid? Now we're *both* down here." "Yeah," says the second man, "but I've been down here before, and I know the way out."[1]

In the Incarnation, we celebrate God's jumping into the *hole* of our humanity and into the *whole* of our humanity, with all its joy and pain. We have reason to hope, after all, in an unrelentingly fearful world, that the angels' message makes sense after all. We

---

1. "Noel," *The West Wing* (Warner Bros. Television/NBC, December 20, 2000).

can "fear not," because we know and worship a God who's been down here before and knows the way back up to the Light.

It's not that God will make everything all right. God never promised to take away all the pain, either that inflicted by an Osama bin Laden from afar, or the pain inflicted by those we love near at hand. But this God promises to be with us to the end of the age. Our joy and fulfillment don't depend on the size of our portfolio or the size of our waistline, nor on the economy nor on our jobs. Our confidence isn't destroyed with the collapse of towers of steel and concrete, or by explosions in railway stations. Our hope is undiminished because our God is with us. That's the mystery and miracle of the Incarnation. And that's why those angels knew what they were talking about when they said, "Fear not."

✳ 8 ✳

THE GAMBLE OF FORGIVENESS

Maybe a card game seems like an obscene image to use when talking about the crucifixion, but when you think about it, it's very apt. In a card game, if you're smart, you keep a poker face and never let your opponents know what you're thinking or what you're planning to do. Whether you've got a full house or a bust, you never let on. And above all else, you play your cards close to your chest, careful not to tip your hand and reveal your true strength or weakness, lest you be taken advantage of.

What we learn as we witness Jesus on the cross is that God is a lousy card player. No poker face here. Jesus, as he has done his whole life, and finally on the cross, lays all God's cards on the table for everyone to see. God's hand is tipped for all eternity. Watch carefully as God refuses to play his cards close to his chest, refuses to hide who he is, refuses to be careful about being taken advantage of.

"Father, forgive them, for they know not what they do," Jesus says in the midst of his agony. Forgiveness is at the heart of what's happening on the cross, at the heart of what's being accomplished once and for all. The gap that exists between us and God — a distance we've created by our self-centeredness and our hardness of heart and our thoughtlessness — is bridged on the cross by God, right up to our doorstep.

It's no surprise, really. Jesus is saying and doing what he's always said and done. "I tell you, you must forgive seventy times seven," he instructed his followers. Instead of throwing a stone at the woman caught in adultery, he offers her a new life. And nowhere does God lay his cards on the table more clearly than in the parable of the prodigal son, which, of course, isn't so much a story about the prodigal son as it is about the loving, forgiving Father.

The son goes off, creating a distance between himself and his father, unaware of what he's doing, oblivious to the damage he's doing to his soul. And the father sits on the porch, day after day, eyes straining to see down the road, hoping against hope for the son's return; sitting in his rocking chair, tears streaming down his face at the pain his son undoubtedly has come to know; holding no grudge. He's already forgiven the son. He's only praying for his return.

One day, of course, the son wakes up and realizes what he's done. But before he can even begin to make his apology and beg his Father's forgiveness, the Father has run down the road to embrace him, welcome him home, and throw a big party to celebrate his return.

That's precisely what happens on the cross — and it's happening for you and me, right now, at every moment. God is laying all of God's cards on the table. You want to know how much God loves you? Look at the cross. You want to know whether or not God forgives all your sins? Look at the cross. You want to see God running toward you, arms outstretched, ready to embrace you and throw a party in your honor? Look at the cross.

There's only one catch. There's one part of this drama that you and I have to supply. God has done everything else. God has offered God's self and forgiven our sins. The only thing we have to do is believe and accept that forgiveness.

Karl Menninger, a famous psychiatrist, once said that if he could convince the patients in psychiatric hospitals that their sins were forgiven, three-quarters of them could walk out the next day. Odd as it may sound, accepting the forgiveness accomplished and demonstrated on the cross is scary. To leave our sins at the foot of the cross might free us to do remarkable, but difficult, things. If we let go of all the heavy baggage we're toting around, God might ask us to use our now-free hands to love the world. And underneath it all, if we're really honest, we may not be really sure of our own worth, not sure that we shouldn't pay for our sins, not sure that God could be *that* forgiving.

But look at the cross. God is forgiving not just those who "know not what they do." God is also forgiving those who know exactly what they're doing. It's at the moment we realize who we are and what we've done — and that we are loved anyway — that we experience the forgiveness of the cross. It's not that we finally forgive ourselves, we just don't have the power to do that. But we can, by the grace of God, allow ourselves to accept the forgiveness God offers us from the cross.

When I was growing up in Kentucky, in a little rural church too poor to afford air conditioning, the local funeral homes would provide the church with fans, and on stifling summertime Sundays, we'd use them to stir the hot, humid air that filled the place. On most of those fans was the picture of a sappy, effeminate, Anglo-Saxon, blond-haired, blue-eyed Jesus, standing outside a heart-shaped door, knocking.

The picture may have been a little tacky, and it certainly didn't portray Jesus as the Jew he was, but the message was exactly right. Our sins are forgiven. Already, before we ask. God has traveled and bridged the great distance that separates us from him and from one another. On the cross, God has shown his hand and proclaimed to us just how much he loves us. And we have a choice: we can hold on to our sins and let them continue to weigh us down and limit the ways we can serve one another. Or we can do God the greatest honor by leaving those sins at the foot of the cross. All we have to do is show our cards, just as God does. All we have to do is open that door to our hearts, accept the forgiveness God has already won for us, and let the party begin.

❊ 9 ❊

HEART'S DESIRE

Let's face it: Christians prefer the nice stories about Jesus: the images of him walking on the water, calming the storm, feeding the multitude. But *pow!* — right in the middle of our stories about Nice Jesus comes the story of Scary Jesus: in the Gospel of John, the healer, the miracle-worker, the all-around nice guy starts making claims about himself that we just don't hear in the other Gospels, even going so far as to say that the bread he has to give is his flesh. No wonder some pagans and people of other faiths have wondered if we Christians were a cannibalistic cult.

But what do we make of these troublesome proclamations? What does the Jesus of John's Gospel call us to do? It seems more like troubling news than good news.

First, consider the source. The Gospel of John isn't much interested in the events of Jesus' life, per se, but with what those events mean. It begins not with Jesus' birth, but goes way, way back: "In the beginning was the Word, and the Word was with God, and the Word was God" (John 1:1). It's a bit like reading the last, revealing page of a murder mystery first. John wants you to know right from the get-go who this Jesus is. John's is the only Gospel without an account of the institution of the Lord's Supper, but pages and pages of the conversation that happened there. John's Gospel is an expression of the way the early Christian community understood what the events in Jesus' life meant for them at the end of the first century. Modern scholars debate to this day how much of the real, earthly Jesus is found in this Gospel, and how

much is an account of the way the early church experienced —
and related to — the risen Lord half a century later.

And what those first-century Christians wanted to know, after
they heard about Jesus feeding five thousand people with a couple
of loaves and fishes, was "What does this mean?"

Jesus always drew on familiar images, which made him popular and accessible to the people who heard him. Hunger and
thirst were understood by everyone, especially these descendants
of the ancient Hebrews, whose cultural and religious history was
wrapped up with wandering in the desert, dependent on God for
water and manna. No wonder we remember so vividly so many of
Jesus' actions and images tied up with hunger and thirst, not just
the feeding of the multitude, but his changing water into wine at
a wedding in Cana, his talking with the woman at the well about
living water, his offering of bread and wine at the Last Supper.

But when Jesus fed those five thousand people, they — and the
disciples too — missed the point. Their bellies full, they focused
on the temporary, superficial hunger that could be satisfied with
a fish dinner. But for Jesus, the focus was on a deeper hunger
that couldn't be filled by mere food, but could be satisfied only
by God.

Being fed is a very nice image that we all understand. But go a
little deeper, and you'll see that this story calls us to a powerful
and important spiritual journey.

An incident in the fictional life of Harry Potter comes to mind.
In the first book of the series, Harry begins his first year at Hog-
warts, a school for magicians. After hair-raising twists and turns
of the plot, Harry finds himself in an empty room with "a magnificent mirror, as high as the ceiling, with an ornate gold frame,
standing on two clawed feet." Looking into the mirror, he's horrified, at first, to see other faces in the mirror alongside his own,
and he realizes they're the faces of his long-dead mother and
father and other relatives. And to this boy who was orphaned
as a baby, it's a long-hoped-for miracle. Gazing into the mirror

satisfies something deep within him that's gnawed at him like a terrible hunger. Later, when Harry brings his friend Ron Weasley to the secret room to see his family in the mirror, his friend sees something quite different. It takes Professor Dumbledore, one of the teachers at the school, to explain that this enchanted mirror "shows us nothing more or less than the deepest, most desperate desire of our hearts."[1]

If we're to grow as Christians, if we want to understand the meaning of Jesus' words about the bread of life, then we too must look into the mirror and discover the deepest, most desperate desire of our hearts. It is not unlike the question that Jesus posed to nearly every single person who came to him: "What do you want? What do you want?"

So think for a moment, right now, about what you want, what you really want, what you long for most, what you hunger and thirst for, what you most deeply desire. When you look in the enchanted mirror, what do you see? Don't discard anything that comes to your mind because you think it might be too trivial or too crass and material or not holy enough or worthy enough. These first images that come to mind may point to your real heart's desire.

The new house I long for may point to my need and longing for a spiritual home inside the physical house that is nurturing and supportive, a haven of peace. That flashy red sports car may point to my mid-life crisis and my need to feel young and productive and vibrant again — professionally, personally, or even sexually. My worrying about needing just a bit more money in the bank may point to my need for security and confidence in my old age. My wanting a different job, a different spouse, a different life may point to my underlying disappointment in myself and my anxiety over not having made the most out of my life. My drive to run for office, get another degree, be the chair of the department, achieve

---

1. J. K. Rowling, *Harry Potter and the Sorcerer's Stone* (New York: Scholastic, 1997), 213.

another goal may point to my never having felt affirmed and accepted as I am, whether by my parents, my spouse or partner, or my colleagues.

Beneath each one of these desires lies a deeper spiritual need. That's what Jesus knew as he fed the five thousand, and that's what he wanted his disciples to understand. The bread of this world would never ease the deep hunger they felt. Push the hunger far enough, deep enough, and you come up with a spiritual need, a spiritual longing, that no earthly bread will satisfy.

This is spiritual work that we're all called to do. Looking into the mirror and seeing our heart's deepest desire is hard and very scary. Who knows what we'll see? Who knows what we'll be called upon to do? Who knows what we'd find if we stopped and looked deeply into ourselves?

What would it be like for you and me to focus on what we desire and long for? And then not to settle just for the easy, obvious, superficial answers that would seem to satisfy our longing — like a loaf of fresh bread — but to sit quietly with our longing, to be in God's presence with our deepest desires, to acknowledge our longing, to let God feed that hunger with the bread of life. What would it be like to believe, to truly believe, that those who ask will receive?

This is scary spiritual work. Who knows where it will lead? Who knows what God will ask of us? Who knows what we'll be called to do to satisfy our own hunger? We might have to give up something we've always thought was important to us. We might have to abandon a long sought-after goal — or take up a new one. We might finally be called to give up on a relationship — or open ourselves to another one. We might have to face an addiction and start on the road to recovery. We might have to swallow our pride or admit we're wrong, to heal a broken relationship with a child or sibling or parent. We might begin to realize that true security comes only from a life lived in God. We might begin to give our spiritual lives the attention they deserve.

I don't know where all this might lead, but I believe we are called to it. Not to be embarrassed by our deepest desires, but to embrace and explore them and then seek the Holy One who is the bread of life and who can feed our deepest hunger.

"I am the living bread," says Jesus. Not like the manna in the desert or the loaves and fishes, which offer only temporary relief. "I am living bread," he tells us. "Whoever eats this bread will live forever." Jesus promises that if we seek, we will find; if we knock, it will be opened to us. If we boldly acknowledge and seek our deepest desire, we will be found, and fed, by God. We can continue trying to satisfy our hunger with worldly, temporary things, or we can go deeper and be fed the bread of life.

What is your heart's deepest desire? What do you really want?

✻ 10 ✻

I LOVE TO TELL
THE STORY

I love to tell the story, 'twill be my theme in glory,
To tell the old, old story of Jesus and His love.

Are you saved?

Maybe you can pinpoint the moment it happened. Or maybe you just get irritated when a perfect stranger asks you that question. But the most important thing any of us can learn to do — in church or school or the office or the mall — is to tell the story of our own salvation. When people come to talk to me, wondering about what it is that God wants them to do, I tell them that above and beyond everything else, the first thing they need to do is to tell, in their own words, the story that's recounted in the sixth chapter of Isaiah:

> In the year that King Uzziah died, I saw the Lord sitting on a throne, high and lofty; and the hem of his robe filled the temple. Seraphs were in attendance above him; each had six wings: with two they covered their faces, and with two they covered their feet, and with two they flew. And one called to another and said:
>
> > "Holy, holy, holy is the LORD of hosts;
> > the whole earth is full of his glory."
>
> The pivots on the thresholds shook at the voices of those who called, and the house filled with smoke. And I said:

"Woe is me! I am lost, for I am a man of unclean lips, and I live among a people of unclean lips; yet my eyes have seen the King, the Lord of hosts!" Then one of the seraphs flew to me, holding a live coal that had been taken from the altar with a pair of tongs. The seraph touched my mouth with it and said: "Now that this has touched your lips, your guilt has departed and your sin is blotted out." Then I heard the voice of the Lord saying, "Whom shall I send, and who will go for us?" And I said, "Here am I; send me!" (Isa. 6:1–8)

This story contains all the elements of the call to ministry that each Christian receives at baptism. So "Are you saved?" is a fair question for each of us. But don't stop there. What's the story of your salvation? What's your vision of God? Your answers may not involve falling off a horse, or gazing upon angels on clouds with harps. But what *is* your vision? It's a vision you need to be able to articulate. To be an effective witness in the world, you need words. You need the words to tell your unique story of salvation. You need language to describe your vision of holiness.

Reality check: In all honesty, how close have you come to that vision of holiness — and how far have you fallen short? Knowing that, none of us can ever say anything but "I am so, so unworthy"? Unworthiness was no excuse for Isaiah, and it's no excuse for us.

Like Isaiah, we're all people of "unclean lips." We're all in this together. But for Isaiah, and for us, God does this astounding thing. God takes a burning-hot live coal, touches it to our lips, and takes our sin away. So whatever way we've been called to minister, we need to ponder this: How were my *my* lips touched by that burning-hot coal? What is *my* experience of being saved by God? How have *I* experienced being loved, despite everything I am, despite my failings and shortcomings? In what sense have I been saved — and then what did I do about it?

That's the heart of the matter. That feel-good sense of my own personal salvation is never enough. Not according to God. God, who always has something in mind for us to do — our ministry — has always been saying, "Oh yeah, and by the way, who will go for me? Whom shall I send?"

The answer, in one way or another, is always you and me. As Christians, we're called to take risks for the Gospel, to get into some Gospel trouble. If we ever find ourselves in trouble for preaching the Gospel in words or actions, then we can be pretty sure we're on the right track. Jesus, after all, was always in trouble for preaching the Gospel. If we're moving along without causing too much of a disturbance, then we need to ask ourselves this: "Am I *really* living the Gospel? Am I really telling my salvation story?"

After all, the story of our salvation is really the only story we have to tell. It's the story of how the God of all creation cared enough to save us *and* save the world. Whether we were a kid from the streets or a kid from the wealthy suburbs, we've got to be able to say how God has impacted our life. And then, once we've told that story to someone else, let God do the rest. We don't have to do anything but witness to what God has done for us. We surely don't have to tell others what God has to do for *them.* God will take care of that.

The scriptures are part of our story too. We need to make them our own, to reclaim those stories as *our* stories. This is especially important for gay and lesbian people who have been told for countless generations that scripture — in only about seven places — proves that we're bad. But I find myself in plenty of other places in the Bible. All of us need to find ourselves in the wonderful, rich stories of scripture.

Consider the Exodus story, one of the greatest coming-out stories in the history of the world. You may think about whatever prison you find yourself in, but gay and lesbian people know this story, know what it's like to be in slavery. We know what it's like to be told we're worth nothing, and what it's like to have a Moses show up and say, "They're wrong. You not only deserve to be free from slavery, but God has in mind for you a promised land beyond anything you've ever imagined."

Some of us have been courageous enough to act on that good news, but when we get to the Red Sea — there are always bound to be obstacles along the way — we expect it to be just like Cecil B. De Mille's *Ten Commandments:* the water opens up and a nice dry path forms all the way across. But it usually doesn't work like that. When we get to the Red Sea, it only parts enough for just one footfall. And then it parts just enough for the next footfall, and then the next. We have to put one foot down and take a leap of faith every step of the way, without seeing the other side, without knowing exactly what awaits us. For gay and lesbian people, when you come out — and for all of us when we take a courageous new direction in our lives — we don't get to the other side the next day. We wander in the desert for a good long while.

But the desert is a very special, crucial, and necessary place because it's where we become totally dependent on God, who cares for us in unexpected ways and feeds us with manna from heaven. The manna may taste like wet cardboard, but it teaches us about relying on God for our very lives. In the incredibly dark time after I'd come out and separated from my wife, I felt so close to those ancient Hebrews. I didn't know if I could make it through each day, and when I'd go to bed at night, I only had two things: my integrity and God. But I learned that that was just enough. And so we move on for a long time before we approach the promised land.

I don't think you can get to the real promised land until you get to heaven. That was true for Abraham: as the Book of Hebrews recounts, he dreamed of a city with firm foundations, but he just wasn't meant to live there. Instead, he had to learn to dwell in tents, living a nomadic existence and trusting in God for his security. It's true for us, too. All of us were meant to wander in the

desert, learning that life is more about the journey than the des-
tination and that in the end, God will bring us to heaven. We're
all coming out from something. We're all of us children trying to
come out of our various prisons and find our way home. We find
ourselves in the scripture stories that encourage us and inspire us
and help us tell our very own stories about our own salvation.

And since we're telling stories, let's pay attention to the characters, not just the plot. Think of the people that Jesus paid attention
to, and make sure those people are part of your story too. If we're
to be followers of Jesus we have to become passionate about the
people and things that Jesus was passionate about, even though
he was killed because of it. Consider these verses from Isaiah
61:1–2:

> The spirit of the Lord God is upon me,
> because the Lord has anointed me;
> he has sent me to bring good news to the oppressed,
> to bind up the brokenhearted,
> to proclaim liberty to the captives,
> and release to the prisoners;
> to proclaim the year of the Lord's favor

These are the people Jesus cared about — the people on the
margins. Jesus made a habit of releasing people from prison.
Those who lived in the prison of leprosy, the terrifying disease
of his time. Can you imagine what it was like to have Jesus walk
up and touch you, knowing that he was making himself ritually unclean? Can you imagine what that did for the souls of the
people he touched? Those who lived in the prison of gender, re-
viled just for being a woman. Can you imagine having Jesus treat
you not like a piece of meat, not like somebody to be bartered
and married off, but like a human being? No wonder women
followed him everywhere and supported his ministry personally
and financially. No wonder they were the ones at the foot of the

cross when everybody else ran like crazy. No wonder they were the first witnesses to the resurrection.

Hanging around with people like that — the despised of his time and culture — it's no wonder Jesus got into trouble.

You and I could get into that kind of Gospel trouble. But for that to happen, we've got to focus on the Gospel and not a host of other distractions. The debate about whose sexuality is acceptable may be just a way to avoid talking about ministering in the way Jesus did. If we keep talking about what people do in bed, or who ought to get married, or which celebrity is in rehab and why, we don't have to talk about ourselves and the things that really matter in our culture and our society — racism and homophobia, injustice and war. We'll find ourselves in hot water if we start making connections between what the Bible says and what our society does. That, after all, is what got Jesus killed. He saw injustice and pointed it out, and he was victorious because he kept pointing it out, even when it landed him on the cross!

We are called to be passionate about the people and the things that Jesus was passionate about — the last, the lost, and the least — or Christianity is just some personal feel-good thing that we've got going on in the church. If we're not making trouble and making waves, then we'd best check to see if we're preaching the same Gospel that Jesus was preaching. It got him in trouble with the religious powers that be, and if we start doing that, we'll be in trouble too. We need to make sure that the characters in our story are pretty much the same characters that were in Jesus' story. Consider this story, from the third chapter of Acts:

> One day Peter and John were going up to the temple at the hour of prayer, at three o'clock in the afternoon. And a man lame from birth was being carried in. People would lay him daily at the gate of the temple called the Beautiful Gate so that he could ask for alms from those entering

the temple. When he saw Peter and John about to go into the temple, he asked them for alms. Peter looked intently at him, as did John, and said, "Look at us." And he fixed his attention on them, expecting to receive something from them. But Peter said, "I have no silver or gold, but what I have I give you; in the name of Jesus Christ of Nazareth, stand up and walk." And he took him by the right hand and raised him up; and immediately his feet and ankles were made strong. Jumping up, he stood and began to walk, and he entered the temple with them, walking and leaping and praising God. All the people saw him walking and praising God, and they recognized him as the one who used to sit and ask for alms at the Beautiful Gate of the temple; and they were filled with wonder and amazement at what had happened to him. (Acts 3:1–10)

This story is so important to me as a gay man, and to a lot of other people — people of color, women, people in wheelchairs, all kinds of folks who have been told that they don't belong inside the temple, that the closest they can come is the back door because they're not good enough to come inside.

But Peter and James call out, "We don't have any money, but in the name of Jesus, get up and walk." And this guy not only gets up and walks, but begins to dance and run and leap and play, and he runs inside the temple, where he suspected he belonged all along, and claims it for his own. This story is so important to me because for the first forty years of my life I believed I was an abomination. But in the name of Jesus, someone told that man at the gate, and me, to stand up and walk.

That Gospel story is our story. We belong right in the center of things, and that is very good news. But we don't get to stay there. We have to go out in the streets and find all the people who still think they're not worthy, who still think God couldn't possibly love them, and bring them inside the temple. We need to learn to run and leap and dance and laugh and sing as one of God's own, and invite others to dance too.

This is an inspiring story, of course, and it's all very well and good. But it doesn't come cheap. We need to be prepared to pay a price. The people in the civil rights movement knew they'd pay a price for what they did: water hoses, dogs, jail, or even death. What risks have we taken for the Gospel? What waves are we making?

One of the challenges about being elected bishop — but also one of the blessings — is the cost. Just before my consecration I received a number of death threats. I wore a bulletproof vest at my consecration, and bomb-sniffing dogs made the rounds in the arena that served as our church. My daughters were there, and they were pretty worried about me. But I was able say, "There are a lot of things worse than dying, like not really living, for instance. That would be the real tragedy. If I should die today, you'll know that I was doing what I felt God was calling me to do, and that's the ultimate blessing."

We must be willing to pay a price for telling our story — God's story — and not be surprised by it. We need to prepare one another for it, and if we see people paying that price, we need to support them in the midst of conflict. It goes with the territory.

Conflict is no stranger in my life, but look at what it's done to strengthen my relationship with God. I'd go through it all over again. So let's not be afraid of conflict. Let's look for God in the middle of it.

As ministers of the Gospel, ordained and lay, we're all called to make the Gospel story — the Good News — our own and then to take it to people who don't have the blessing of knowing and believing. There is no end to God's love for us. We don't have to lose hope, we don't have to get discouraged, we don't have to get burnt out, because we're all just doing our little piece, making our small contribution to that forward journey toward the vision of God. And we can all do our little piece because we *all* know how it's going to end. It's going to end with this loving God of ours being absolutely victorious. This God of ours will keep loving us so much, no matter how hardheaded we are, no matter how much we resist God's will. Our God will keep loving us until we are all reconciled with that wonderful God. As the hymn I grew up with says, we must love to "tell the old, old story." It's an old story, but it's our story too, and it's very good news indeed. So the next time somebody asks you, "Are you saved?" try this: Answer with a cheerful "You bet! And have I got a story for you..."

* 11 *

RISKING EVERYTHING

This letter was found in a baking powder can wired to the handle of an old pump that offered the only hope of drinking water on a very long and seldom-used trail across the desert:

> This pump is all right as of June 1932. I put a new sucker washer into it and it ought to last five years. But the washer dries out and the pump has got to be primed. Under the white rock I buried a bottle of water, out of the sun and cork end up. There's enough water in it to prime the pump, but not if you drink some first. Pour about one fourth and let her soak to wet the leather. Then pour in the rest medium fast and pump like crazy. You'll git water. The well has never run dry. Have faith. When you git watered up, fill the bottle and put it back like you found it for the next feller.
>
> [signed] Desert Pete
>
> P.S. Don't go drinkin' up the water first. Prime the pump with it, and you'll git all you can hold."[1]

The parable of the talents is a lot like the note left by Desert Pete. Both the note and the parable talk about life and how it is to be lived — boldly, and on faith. They both also point to the consequences of not living that way. Both the parable and the story of Desert Pete proclaim that boldness and faith are matters of life and death.

---

1. See Keith Miller and Bruce Larson, *The Edge of Adventure: Finding What's Real While Looking for God* (Waco, Tex.: Word Books, 1974).

It would be easy, I guess, to read this parable of the talents as an allegory, trying to connect each character and action with some specific person or group. But Jesus rarely tells his stories that way, detail by detail. Usually, he just makes one point, teaches one lesson. The trick, of course, is figuring out exactly what that is.

Here's the "Cliff's Notes" version of the story: There's a master who goes off on a long trip, but before he leaves, he entrusts his servants with great responsibility, leaving them free to act or not to act on the master's behalf and in his name. He gives each of the three servants a sum of money and challenges them to invest it, earning more for the master. If this were a TV reality show, Donald Trump would play the part of the master, and somebody would get fired at the end.

Each servant gets a different amount of money. Two of the servants take their seed money, risk it, and make a tidy profit. When the master returns, he rewards them lavishly: "Enter into the joy of your master," he declares.

But the third servant was a cautious, risk-averse guy, and instead of investing his money, he dug a hole and buried it in his garden. He's in for a big surprise when he returns the money — intact and unchanged — without even the interest he might have earned in a savings account at the bank or from lending the money out. The angry, disappointed master takes even that bit of treasure away.

The master, of course, isn't just like God in every way. This guy, after all, isn't only angry and harsh, but a little manipulative too. And the point of the story isn't that the rich get richer and the poor get poorer, and God sets it up that way.

Perhaps instead, it's about this: the Christian life has more to do with investing than with saving, more to do with risking than with protecting, more to do with living with boldness than with proceeding with caution.

But like the master in this story, God entrusts us with responsibility and leaves us free to act — and free not to act — in God's name. And like the three servants, people have different gifts and talents and capabilities. Some of us are enormously gifted; most of us only moderately so — though we all tend to underestimate the wealth of riches we've been given.

But the first two servants risk all they have been given in the hopes of being good stewards of the riches entrusted to them. Though they earn different amounts, their commitment is similar, and they're invited to share in their master's joy. The third servant — and he is clearly the focus of the story and the most likely to make us squirm — fails because, as he admits, he was afraid.

The third servant went wrong in another way as well. He really didn't *know* his master. Instead of brimming with excitement about the joy the master was eager to share, he cowered in fear, with the mistaken thought that the master was vindictive, cruel, even dishonest. Locked in his own fear, he was helpless to use his blessings creatively and constructively. He let his riches dissipate from non-use, like a muscle that atrophies when it's not exercised.

Maybe we've let our treasures atrophy, too. However much or little we've been given, the question for us is the same as it was for the three servants: "What will I do with what I've been given?" And: "What kind of master do I serve?" It makes a big difference.

Do we know our Master? Do we know God as the gracious giver of all blessings, entrusting to us the necessary gifts for an abundant and joyful life? Or are we, as New England preacher Jonathan Edwards used to say, merely "sinners in the hands of an angry God"?[2] Do we think of ourselves as co-creators with God, using our gifts to be God's loving arms in the world, no matter the risk or cost? Or are we fearful and timid, afraid to risk losing what little we think we have and expecting a capricious and punitive God to swoop in to punish and rebuke? Knowing

---

2. Title of a sermon preached in Enfield, Connecticut, July 8, 1741.

the master makes a lot of difference in how we live our lives as Christians.

This is the way Jesus lived his life. This theme — that life is to be given, spent, invested, not held on to — runs through his life and ministry. "If any want to become my followers," Jesus declares, "let them deny themselves and take up their cross and follow me. For those who want to save their life will lose it, and those who lose their life for my sake will find it. For what will it profit them if they gain the whole world but forfeit their life?" (Matt. 16:24–26) Take up your cross, risk your life, take a chance on losing whatever you fear losing the most, and follow me.

It's not just about life's big decisions. It's also about taking risks with simple, day-to-day things. It's a risk to make a phone call or write a note to someone you're angry with, someone who's hurt you: depending on the response you get, you're at risk for more hurt and a battered ego. It's a risk to visit a friend who's sick or dying: you might be embarrassed by not knowing what to say. It's a risk to discipline a child fairly and consistently: you might fear losing the child's love. It's a risk to confront a spouse, friend, or co-worker about an unspoken-but-ever-present problem: you might lose the facade of peace and harmony. It's a risk to join AA, to go for counseling, to get into therapy, to face your own demons courageously: you might fail and have to start all over again from scratch, more hopeless than before.

What I've learned in my life — and perhaps it squares with what you've learned in yours — is that abundant and joyful life rarely accompanies "playing it safe." The life we've been given by God is a treasure to be invested, not to be possessed, to be risked, rather than to be buried in the ground or hidden under a mattress. The writer of Psalm 23, who proclaims "my cup runneth over," has found that joy only after walking "through the valley of the shadow of death." Each of us must decide whether we'll invest our lives or squirrel them away.

The good news is that we're not alone. When we take that risk and when we find ourselves in the valley of the shadow of death, we will be comforted and sustained. As Bishop Barbara Harris is fond of saying, "The power behind you is greater than the task before you." When we're in the desert, we can count on manna from God.

So back to the parable of Desert Pete and the well. Our loving master has left us lots of notes at the well. The Gospel story of the talents is one of them. Everything we need for finding living water and abundant life has been provided — *except* that we need to take a risk to retrieve it. Like the servant who had to invest his money rather than bury it, we who stand at the well in the desert have to pour every drop of precious water into the pump, and then pump like crazy. Risk-taking like that is hard to do when it's hot and dry and we're thirsty beyond belief.

But our lives, like the bottle of water and the talents in the parable, are to be invested, risked, not possessed. The unnerving and frightening message of the story of the talents is that not only will there come an accounting for how we've lived our lives, but also that whatever reward or punishment for the life we lead begins now. If we bury our treasure underground or put it in a sock under the mattress, we won't find much that's invigorating and enlivening in our lives, and the world that so desperately needs us and needs God's love will remain in need.

Or we can stake our whole being on life as something to be risked, invested, something we can win only if we're willing to lose it. And in the process we'll probably find that it's only in the risking and giving of ourselves that we're invited into the joy of the master and the abundant life he promises.

When we find Desert Pete's bottle of water in our own deserts, we can be so fearful of trusting the promise of the well that we drink the bottle of water for ourselves, momentarily quenching our thirst, but then finding ourselves facing the desert alone and without resources. Or we can trust the author of the note and the promise of the well that's never run dry, pour the last drops of precious water into the pump, pump like crazy, and find more living water than we can imagine.

Whatever we're being called to risk right now in our lives, big or small, the God of life and the author of our salvation is with us. However we're called to invest our lives rather than save them, we should remind ourselves that we're not alone, and that the power behind us is greater than the task before us. No matter what uncertainties we face, we can trust that this well of God's grace and goodness has never — and will never — run dry.

Part Three

EMBRACING THE EXILE

Notes from the Margins

Look with pity, O heavenly Father, upon the people in this land who live with injustice, terror, disease, and death as their constant companions. Have mercy upon us. Help us to eliminate our cruelty to these our neighbors. Strengthen those who spend their lives establishing equal protection of the law and equal opportunities for all. And grant that every one of us may enjoy a fair portion of the riches of this land; through Jesus Christ our Lord. Amen.

— Prayer for the Oppressed,
The Book of Common Prayer, p. 826

J ESUS SPENT much of his time with the marginalized. Can you imagine what it was like to be a leper, despised and feared by all, forced to shout a warning when anyone came near, abandoned to live in caves or graveyards — and then to have your face touched and your heart moved by the itinerant preacher and holy man from Nazareth?

If we are to be followers of Jesus and not just his admirers, then we must do the things Jesus did with the marginalized people he did them with. In seeking out and speaking out for those who find themselves on the edges of society and respectability, we come close to the Jesus we follow. Jesus reminds us that it is not those who merely call him Lord who are acceptable to God, but rather those who work for justice and do the will of God.

✻ 12 ✻

WE ARE THE CHURCH

For an institution that prides itself on helping people to be good, the church has done much for which it should repent. Examples abound. Consider, for example, that it took four hundred years to admit that Galileo, not the church, was right about the earth's orbit around the sun.

That's ancient history, you say? Well, let's be honest. To this day, the teachings of the church, synagogue, and mosque continue to be the source of the greatest oppression of gays and lesbians. Portions — though very few and far between portions — of our holy texts have been understood literally and out of context and used to oppress people. It's not something new in the history of religion, but that doesn't make it any less painful or destructive. People of African descent in the United States lived for years with the horrific institution of slavery, a sin against God and humankind that was bolstered and supported, said its proponents, by scripture. By the grace of God and the leading of the Holy Spirit, faith communities came to realize that people of color were children of God, equal in dignity and worth to every other child of God. For years the churches of the Anglican Communion discriminated against women, denying them their equal place in lay leadership and in the ranks of the clergy. Many churches, synagogues, and mosques still believe that such discrimination is God's will, and point to scripture to prove it. It seems inconceivable now that it's been only a few decades since the Episcopal Church began to allow women to serve as deputies to our General Convention and to ordain women to the priesthood and the episcopate.

God didn't get things wrong. The church got things wrong. It's a reminder that the church is a human institution, trying its very best to discern the will of the Living God in its own time and place. Discerning the will of God, especially when it flies in the face of what we've always believed, is hard, and sometimes it takes us a long time to figure it out.

But God is doing a new thing in the church, the synagogue, the mosque, and the world. Just as God has led us to a new understanding about people of color, women, and the differently abled, so too is God leading us to challenge the long-accepted notions about the place of gay and lesbian people in the church and in the world.

And since religious belief and teaching are the source of the oppression of the lgbt community, it's going to take religious people to undo that thinking and believing. The lgbt community needs to make allies in the religious communities who speak religious language, who are not afraid to argue knowledgeably about these passages of scripture in light of all of scripture, and who exhibit Christian belief and virtue in their own lives so that old understandings give way to new.

And whether you're religious or not, if you're gay, lesbian, bisexual, or transgendered, you're going to face discrimination based on religion. It's out there in the culture in which all of us live. A few years ago, I helped found an organization for lgbt and questioning twelve-to-twenty-one-year-olds. One evening, the discussion turned to God, and although not one of these kids had grown up in a religious home, they all thought they knew what God thought of them. They couldn't have found Leviticus in the Bible if their lives had depended on it — they probably had never heard of Leviticus — but they knew the word "abomination," and they thought this was the way God regarded them. The self-loathing, the fear, and the sense of being "less than" in the eyes of God were central to the way they understood themselves as gay or lesbian. Not only were they misunderstood and criticized by their parents and friends, but even God thought they were defective and sinful. This undoubtedly contributes to the suicides and attempted suicides so prevalent among gay teens. Changing this understanding is literally a life and death issue for all of us as a community.

It's also why Harvey Milk, the first openly gay supervisor in the city of San Francisco, who was assassinated in 1978 by an anti-gay colleague, insisted that "the most political thing any of us can do is come out." It is also the most religious thing we can do. The reason, the only reason, religious groups of all kinds are now struggling with the issue of homosexuality is that sons and daughters, relatives, friends, and co-workers — and now even bishops — have come out. Because we are loved already and because we are valued in our religious communities, our coming out raises the question of whether or not we can be both a person who is gay and a person of faith. Believers in every religious community — even those who are absolutely clear about their negative stance on lgbt people — are beginning to ask, "How can it be that this fine, faithful contributor to our religious community can be an abomination before God?" Along with Jesus, we ask, "Can a bad tree produce good fruit?" And so in the United States, in Canada, in the United Kingdom — indeed, all over the world — every denomination of the church is struggling with and divided over this issue. Most are asking the hard question: Did we get this wrong?

The Anglican Communion, of course, is deeply divided over this issue. The Episcopal Church in the United States has been lambasted across the globe for consenting to my election as a bishop of the church — a proud gay man, living in a partnered relationship with another man, not afraid to claim God's blessing on my life and ministry as a gay man and a child of God. More and more of us are coming to believe that the few scripture passages that seem to condemn homosexuality are culturally- and

time-bound and make no sense in relation to the whole of scripture. More and more of us are coming to believe that when Jesus
said that God calls all unto God, he meant all — not just some.
Or as Archbishop Desmond Tutu puts it: "All, all, all, all, all!"[1]
In the Canadian Diocese of New Westminster, Bishop Michael
Ingham and his diocese are similarly being lambasted around the
world for blessing the union of two same-gender loving people.
Bishop Ingham and his people may be wondering why, if we can
bless fox hunts and fishing fleets, we cannot bless two people who
pledge to love one another in a faithful, monogamous, life-long-
intentioned union and who seek the church's blessing on that holy
endeavor.

Globally, there is much more going on than the interpretation
of scripture, of course. Those who lead religious communities
in the Global South are rightly angered by the Global North's
domination in recent centuries, marked by colonialism, racism
and disgraceful treatment of those perceived to be less than their
Northern Hemisphere brothers and sisters. And in a world in
which America swaggers around the globe like a cowboy gone
mad, having its way whenever and wherever it wants with no regard for others, our consecration of a gay American bishop and
our blessing of same-sex unions are seen as acts of North American unilateralism and defiance of the cultural sensibilities of our
brothers and sisters in Christ, especially those in the Global South.

But the real problem goes deeper than scripture passages,
deeper than cultural chasms. When you dig down a little more,
you'll find that what we're seeing is the beginning of the end
of patriarchy. For a very long time, men — mostly white, educated, Western, heterosexual men from the Global North — have
been making all the decisions for the world. People of color have
demanded a place at that decision-making table, and so have
women. Now that we lgbt people are claiming a place too, the

---

1. Address at American University, March 18, 2004.

system of patriarchy, out of which all of our Abrahamic religions developed, seems to be starting to unravel. No wonder there's so much resistance! That's why the conservatives are right in saying this is such a big deal. It's not because gay and lesbian people are any different than others who have demanded equality, but because for religious bodies and for the culture, the full equality of gays and lesbians strikes at the very heart of the patriarchy and misogyny that's been the way of the world for so long. And it's why the fights to end racism and sexism, and the struggle to eliminate discrimination against lgbt folk, are so closely intertwined. And it's why, as people of faith, we all need to work together. These interlocking oppressions are all pieces of the same injustice quilt.

So what to do? Three things for starters: first, if you've left your church, synagogue, or mosque, go back or — because congregations are uneven in their treatment of lgbt people — at least come back to a congregation that's willing to accept you as the child of God you were created to be. Your religion needs your voice, needs your witness. And the lgbt community needs the support of the religions that have traditionally condemned it.

Second, come out! Come out as a person of faith to your gay friends, which may be harder than coming out as a gay person to your straight friends! For a lot of good reasons, there's a lot of ill feeling in the gay community against religious groups. To many, asking gay folk to return to church is like asking an abused wife to return to her abusive husband. But lgbt people must reclaim their rightful and God-given place in religious communities and proclaim this message to our gay and lesbian teenagers and to those who come after us: we are loved by God beyond our wildest imagining, and no one, not even religious leaders, can ever take that away.

Third, be willing to pay a price for moving forward. Of course it will be hard. But these are important battles to fight, and

sacrifice and risk-taking on behalf of the Word of God has always been a part of our religious belief and understanding. Jesus
teaches in the beatitudes from the Sermon on the Mount that
"blessed are those who are persecuted for righteousness' sake"
(Matt. 5:10). Instead of giving up on our religious communities, let's think about taking the risks and bearing the burdens
of transforming them.

There is a passage in the Christian scriptures (Acts 3:1–11)
that helps me do that. It takes place soon after the resurrection of
Jesus, and the early Christian community is beginning to notice
that all sorts of undesirable people are responding to the message
of hope they are preaching. All sorts of previously condemned
people are hearing the good news of God and laying claim to it
for themselves.

Peter and John are walking into the temple in Jerusalem, when
they encounter a man everybody knows has been lame since birth;
it was a condition attributed to his own sin or that of his parents.
It made him unacceptable in the eyes of the Law, and it kept him
from entering the temple with all the upstanding worshipers.

This beggar calls out to Peter and John for money, but instead
Peter says, "In the Name of Jesus, stand up and walk." And the
lame man not only stands and walks, but begins running and
leaping and dancing — right into the temple itself. He has claimed
the good news for himself and demands his rightful place — not
at the gate looking in, but inside, claiming God's love.

Gays and lesbians, women and people of color, those who are
differently abled — we all know what it's like to be allowed only
so far inside. We know what it's like to be allowed to come only
so far, but no farther. We all know what it's like to be on the
margins. And we know what it's like to be told that our infirmity
makes us unacceptable to God and to our religious congregation.
But like this man, crippled in body and soul, we too are hearing
God's voice of welcome, claiming the love of God for ourselves
and our lgbt brothers and sisters. We are no longer willing to be

relegated to the outer gates of the temple, but we are living our lives with such joy and hope that the church and the world can no longer doubt the God they see working in us. We will not be excluded from God's love, because God won't have it. And we lay claim to God's blessing — in our lives, our relationships, and in our societies.

The Gospel is about liberation. It's about the blind being made to see, those in prisons being set free, those who thought themselves beyond God's love claiming the divine love that is there for the taking. Gay and lesbian people, like everyone else, need to reconnect their sexuality to their spirituality, and it takes the help of a religious community to do that. Only then will we be whole. The good news is that this is what God wants too, and God stands ready to help if we will but ask. There was a time when "gay Christian" was thought to be an oxymoron. Thank God, yes, thank *God,* those days are over. All of us — gay and straight, black and white, male and female — all of us are the church, and we have claimed our place inside.

✻ 13 ✻

SETTING CAPTIVES FREE

Every year, this is my Christmas present to myself: to spend Christmas Eve with the women of the New Hampshire State Prison for Women.

My relationship with these women began three days after my election. Among the many greetings I received after that event was a note from a woman at the prison. In part it read, "I am neither gay nor Christian, but there is something in your election that makes me believe that there is a community 'out there' who might love me, despite what I've done."

I wanted to get to know this woman and why she had said this. On the day before I left for the General Convention to face the consent process, I went to the New Hampshire State Prison for Women to play softball. And let me tell you, these women play softball! It's as close to a near-death experience as I ever hope to have. I fell over my own feet a few times and left the scene dirty and bloody. But I also fell in love with these women.

And I met the woman who had written the note. She was only eighteen, and she had killed her mother, a forensic psychiatrist, three years earlier. As I talked with her, I got my first inkling about the broad ripples in the lake of humankind my election would cause. She saw in this election — in her eyes, a church choosing an outcast as its leader — hope for her acceptance as a human being despite her heinous crime.

The women at the prison followed my consent process at General Convention on TV, by their account cheering at each victory, horrified at each setback. I went back to visit them after the Convention, and they seemed to know more about what happened there than I did. They made me promise to come back and see them after my consecration — instructing me that they wanted me in all my post-consecration vestments. When I did return to them, dressed to the ecclesiastical nines, they seemed to take great pride, even ownership, in my elevation to the office of bishop.

A year later, during the Advent season, they presented to me a set of "Mary blue" vestments, hand cross-stitched by several of them. "These are Advent vestments," they told me, "because we consider ourselves a community in waiting — waiting for the next visitor, waiting for a parole, waiting for the time when we can leave." On the underneath side of the poncho-like chasuble, the women wrote their names. Though I have many vestments, there are none that I cherish more than these. I promised them that whenever I wore these vestments, I'd tell people about the women in prison.

Why does my relationship with these women mean so much to me? Part of it is that when I'm with them, I feel closer to Jesus. It's not easy to feel close to Christ when you're sitting in a committee meeting or signing papers at a desk. But when you're doing the things that Jesus did with the people he did them with, it's a whole different story. Indeed, visiting those who are in prison is one of the few specific instructions he has given us. And preaching good news to the captives is called for in both Old and New Testaments. Yet for the most part we've forgotten the call to this ministry.

I suppose it would be easy to see my ministry with these women as arrogant and condescending — the holy bishop visiting the wretched and sinful violators of the law. But I feel so blessed when I am with them that I always feel they are the ones who have ministered to *me*. There is perhaps no time when I feel more like a priest, more like a beloved child of God, than when I am permitted the honor of being with these other children of God.

Preaching the good news is easy in this place. These women feel as if the world has forgotten them, that their families and friends are moving on without them. Although they are "doing time," it's almost as if they are suspended outside of time while the world goes on about its business. The image most of them have of themselves is one of failure, low self-esteem, even self-loathing. "How could I have done something so stupid?" they will often ask. Telling them of God's love for them is the very balm they need for their souls, and it is my joy to bring them this good news, which I believe with my whole heart and attempt to demonstrate with my presence.

It's easy to get angry in this place. Many, many of the women in prison are victims of abuse by husbands or boyfriends. After years of ill-treatment, some of it horrific, they simply decided one day to pick up a butcher knife or a gun and end the abuse, without clearly thinking through the consequences of their actions and hardly knowing of any resources that might have offered them a way out that didn't involve violence and eventual incarceration.

Although the State of New Hampshire is the second whitest state in the Union, the women's prison population is disproportionately filled with women of color, a good number of them immigrants. Almost all were poor at the time of their crime, lacking the knowledge and the wherewithal to access the resources that might have helped them. The connections between the "isms" — racism, classism, sexism — are never so clear as in a place like this.

But I like the honesty in this place. There is a low toleration of bulls**t here. The unvarnished truth gets told; emotions are right out on the table. One woman, an immigrant from Venezuela who was brought here by an abusive husband, told me that unlike the world "out there," the women "in here" have no way to hide themselves. "Out there," she told me, "you have clothes and cars and jobs and all kinds of things to mask what is really going on with you. But in here, we all wear the same clothes, there are no cars or jobs, and the only 'stuff' we have is what is on the inside. All we have in dealing with one another is the 'stuff' of our lives." It's why, I guess, I find these women to be so brutally honest with one another and with me. It is both refreshing and frightening to think about living one's life with such honesty.

I have baptized several of these women. It's much like what I imagine baptism to have been like in the early church, with the community of believers gathered around with obvious joy and pride and excitement for the one to be baptized and joined to the community. When was the last time you saw adult baptismal candidates uncontrollably weeping for sheer joy at the thought of God's love for them? When was the last time *we* wept for joy at the simply preposterous notion that Almighty God loves us? No wonder I am inspired by these women.

One of the inmates has joined our local church from inside the walls. She cannot go to services there, but parishioners go to see her and bring tapes of those services. She stitches banners for the church and parish house and keeps up with parish life through the newsletter. (Would that everyone read parish communications with such interest!) One day, when she is very old, having finished a long sentence, she will get to visit St. Matthew's and worship with them physically. Until then, spiritual communion will have to do.

As I write this, it will soon be Christmas Eve again. The women and I will sing everything from "O Holy Night" to "Here Comes Santa Claus" during the hour before the service. And then the Eucharist will begin. And I will begin, once again, to wonder if this isn't the very kind of place God chose to be born as one of us, among the last, the lost, and the least.

There are always tears at this service. Most of these women will not know which of their relatives or friends are caring for their children that night. They will not be putting toys under the tree, or tucking their kids into bed in eager anticipation of Santa's visit. Most of these women will be wondering if anyone is missing them. So when the tender story of a Mother and Child is read, they begin to weep. The prayers are heartbreakingly real and personal. Their prayers are not recitations of beautiful words but desperate pleas to God for deliverance. They are mothers' pleas for God to watch over their children, especially on this night. They are prisoners' pleas for forgiveness. They are human pleas for redemption to the God of all that is.

It is my honor — and my Christmas gift to myself — to be among these, my sisters, on Christmas Eve. It is not only where the bishop ought to be on Christmas Eve; it's where he wants to be. Because sitting among these women, on Christmas Eve, is a little bit like sitting on a hillside in Palestine, alongside the sheep and shepherds, and hearing the most amazing good news of all time: "I bring you good tidings of great joy which shall be for *all* people, even those on the very margins. For unto you is born this day in the City of David, a savior, who is Christ the Lord."

* 14 *

THE NEIGHBORHOOD

My generation was the first to grow up under the threat of nu-clear annihilation. That experience did some frightening things to our self-confidence and changed, in many ways, the way we looked at the world. This is the first generation to grow up facing HIV/AIDS, both on a very personal level and on a societal and global level. In many ways, it's as scary as the threat of nuclear holocaust that hovered over my childhood. But it's also an op-portunity for empowerment. Knowing the risks impels us to take responsibility for our own lives and health and challenges us to look for ways we can make a difference among the neighbors in our communities, and our neighbors out in the world, in response to the crisis of HIV/AIDS.

Jesus tells the story of the Good Samaritan in response to the question: "Who *is* my neighbor?" For people of any faith tradi-tion — or no faith tradition — the story, and the moral embedded within it, that "everyone is my neighbor," is the core of our hu-manity and the key to a compassionate response to HIV/AIDS. For me, as a religious person, it's a call to be God's loving arms in the world.

In the United States, our initial response to AIDS was shame-fully slow, and I think I know why. American society works well for a lot of people, especially those who are white, male, able-bodied, and medically insured. If you're smart and attractive, if you appear to be heterosexual, and if you don't use illicit drugs, so much the better. But if you fall outside one of these categories, life is a little tougher. If you fall outside several of them, you're in big trouble. To look into the face of AIDS is to look into the faces of those people for whom American society — and I suspect other Western societies as well — is *not* working. Along comes this disease that, in the United States, first affected gay and bisexual men and Haitian immigrants, and quickly moved on to IV drug users, people of color in disproportionate numbers, the poor, women, babies, and prostitutes — in short, those on the margins of "respectable" society. It continues to tear through the African American community, especially its women, in this country. Overseas, again it's the women who are hardest hit. It's hard to admit that a society we proudly believe to be egalitarian doesn't care for all its people equally. It's impossible to deal with AIDS and not be confronted by that reality. None of us likes to look at our failures and our injustices, so it's no wonder we don't want to look at AIDS.

As Americans and as religious people, I admit with shame that we were, by choice, far behind other nations in our response to HIV/AIDS. In 1982, several people died after taking Tylenol tablets that had been tampered with. Within *six days*, millions of dollars had been spent in an all-out effort to protect and educate the public about a tragedy that affected just a few people. Legionnaire's disease got swift, thorough attention in the 1970s from every resource available in the federal government, though only a handful of American Legion patriots were affected.

Yet more than forty thousand people were dead of AIDS before the president of the United States ever said the word in public or spent significant money for research or treatment. While the president and Congress congratulated themselves on passing the Ryan White AIDS Care bill in 1990, they provided only partial funding to put it into effect. Why were we so slow to respond? I believe with my whole heart that it's because AIDS first appeared — and continues to appear — in people considered to be dispensable, "throwaway." I can hear the shrill voices now: "Hey, the world would be better off without all those faggots anyway. Nobody forced those drug addicts to stick needles in their arms. So what if this disease threatens to wipe out an entire generation of black and Hispanic people — they're a drain on us anyway, and at least they won't be forever on the welfare rolls!" Though most people are politically correct enough not to articulate such cruel and bigoted sentiments in public, I wonder if those sentiments aren't, for many, just below the surface.

But there are no throwaways in God's kingdom. Not one. We are called by the One who made us to be merciful, loving, and compassionate — not judgmental. We cannot call ourselves good Jews or Christians or Muslims or Hindus, nor even good members of the human race, and then go about our own business doing nothing and "passing by on the other side" as the priest and Levite passed by the man on the side of the road who had been robbed and beaten.

As people of faith, we need to ask of ourselves and our society some tough questions about AIDS and justice, and some of those questions should make us damned uncomfortable. If we're white, we need to explore our own racism, not the kind of obvious, redneck hatred and personal distrust of people of color, but the kind of institutional racism we participate in as white people every day because of the color of our skin, the kind of racism that allows us and our governments not to be terribly worried that we're about to lose huge numbers of people of color to AIDS. If we're well-off financially, we need to ask why poor people don't have jobs, adequate housing, equal education, or accessible health care — never mind why they might turn to drugs or prostitution or crime as ways of coping and then find themselves especially at risk for AIDS. If we're male, we need to see how we benefit in countless ways from the fact that we were born male, and we need to appreciate the incredible burden, including HIV infection, borne by women around the world. If we're heterosexual, we need to wonder why gay and lesbian people continue to be devalued and degraded in public without fear of condemnation from "decent" people. The current debate in the church over the "worth" of gay and lesbian people sadly contributes to this attitude.

But the neighbors we confront in Jesus' parable of the Good Samaritan aren't just the people who live next door. AIDS is no longer an epidemic confined to one country or continent; it is a pandemic infecting and affecting every nation and continent on earth. As in current American society, it is the women of the world who are once again bearing the burden of disease and prejudice. Our neighbors live much farther away than we might have thought.

I had a frightening and wonderful experience in the early 1990s, when I went to Uganda to do AIDS work. Uganda sits on beautiful Lake Victoria, straddling the equator; Winston Churchill called it "the pearl of Africa." And so it was, until Idi Amin and his ruthless collaborators turned it into a twenty-year nightmare. As Ugandans emerged from this reign of terror into the world community, another nightmare had begun.

At that time, in this country of 16 million people, 2 million were already infected with HIV. In the capital, Kampala, one-third were infected. And in the Rakai district, near the Rwandan and Tanzanian border, where HIV first reared its ugly head as a new disease in the world, 50–70 percent were infected. I visited a village inhabited by a couple of eighty-year-old women and a couple of four-year-olds; all the rest were dead. The sugar processing factory had shut down because there is no one left to work in it.

I spent a day in a local clinic with a young doctor whose patients sat or stood for hours in a line that stretched out into the red clay street. When they finally got in to see him, he was able to offer them a kind word, some basic education, and a compassionate touch. He had little more than aspirin for medicine. I sat with some people living with AIDS who were eager to know "the latest" about treatments for their disease; at that time it was AZT, DDI, and the like. I knew, and so did they, that AZT cost thousands of dollars a year and that the average annual income in

Uganda is $240, and I realized that for these people, those drugs might as well never have been invented. The parable of the Good Samaritan goes far beyond taking care of our own.

Doing AIDS work in sub-Saharan Africa is especially complicated, because all the "isms" are at work. You can't do AIDS work without confronting other social problems. I quickly learned that simply to impart information about AIDS and how to prevent it isn't enough. Women at risk for HIV infection because of their husbands' multiple sex partners can't make demands on their husbands without terrible consequences. If she demands that he wear a condom or foreswear his other sexual partners, she can be put out on the street, losing not only her livelihood, but also her children, who "belong" to the husband. HIV/AIDS prevention is tied to ending the patriarchal and sexist privilege that holds these women hostage.

The HIV/AIDS statistics for the global community are difficult to comprehend. Currently, the World Health Organization has estimated that nearly 35 million are infected with HIV, 10 million of them children. Another 10 million children are orphaned. When you remember the profound effect on our global community of the death of 6 million Jews during World War II, it is hard to comprehend the effect of the deaths of so many in this age of AIDS.

Let's come closer to home. Remember that Jesus tells the story of the Good Samaritan in response to the question, "what must I do to inherit eternal life?" The answer is to love God, and to love our neighbor as ourselves. Loving our neighbor begins — and perhaps is only possible — when we love ourselves. So what does loving oneself mean in the age of AIDS?

First, it means being well informed and assuming that all of this applies to us every bit as much as it applies to people in Africa and people who are drug addicts. It means taking this virus very seriously.

Second, it means helping young people to remember that
choosing not to have intercourse is an honorable, positive, and
life-ensuring option in this age of AIDS. It's a choice that allows
them to enjoy their safety, not just from AIDS and pregnancy,
but from the emotional hurt that can easily happen in a sexually
intimate relationship. We can let young people know that there
are wonderful ways of being sexual with another person without
having intercourse, without risking their lives. We may have been
so busy preaching "just say no" that we've forgotten to celebrate
this God-given gift of sexuality and to rejoice in this incredible
means of communicating with a beloved. But there are many ways
of communicating physically and sexually with another person
short of intercourse. And we can teach young people who are
sexually active about safer sex. Their lives may depend upon it.

All of us need to find a way to respond to this disease that goes
beyond ourselves. There are so many people with HIV/AIDS out
there who need our help, and there will be many, many more in
the years to come. Our actions might begin with something as
simple as not tolerating the casual dismissal of those who suffer, to walking in an AIDS walk to raise money for research and
care, to becoming part of a support network for someone living
with AIDS. One of the U.N. Millennium Development Goals is
directed at HIV/AIDS worldwide, and another to the empowerment of women, which will be the key to successful prevention.
Our actions must not end until we have justice for all people.
Love of neighbor demands that we do *something*.

The human community needs all of us in this fight against HIV/
AIDS. Millions of our neighbors around the world will contract
this disease. Some of them live in our town or worship at our
church; most of them live halfway around the world. It doesn't
matter. We need to love each of them, and love ourselves, and be
God's loving arms in the face of this disease. In these people on
the edges we see the face of Christ and learn the meaning of being
a neighbor.

Part Four

GOD'S LOVING HANDS IN THE WORLD

Building the Body of Christ

Almighty God, you proclaim your truth in every age by many voices: Direct, in our time, we pray, those who speak where many listen and write what many read; that they may do their part in making the heart of this people wise, its mind sound, and it will righteous; to the honor of Jesus Christ our Lord. Amen.
— Prayer for Those Who Influence Public Opinion,
The Book of Common Prayer, p. 827

MANY OF US are timid about talking about our faith. The common wisdom is that faith and politics are poor bed-fellows, and everyone knows that religion and politics can ruin a dinner party. But why are mainstream Christians so loath to con-nect their private faith with their public lives? None of us wants to blur the lines the way some on the Religious Right have done, but is that just our excuse for not becoming advocates for justice and peace?

If our faith doesn't inform our lives as citizens of the world, what good is it? The question "What would Jesus do?" should be followed with "What would Jesus buy?" and "Who would Jesus bomb?" The world is in desperate need of our voices for justice and peace, informed and enlightened by our faith. As the old AIDS slogan so aptly puts it, "Silence = Death."

* 15 *

INAUGURATION DAY

Every four years, like clockwork, an army of speechwriters squirrel themselves away in an office in Washington, D.C., and write and re-write and probably write again, an inaugural address for the new president of the United States. It's usually brief, sometimes it's eloquent, and on rare occasions it's even memorable. And whether you agree with the words or not, that inaugural speech tells you where the president's heart is as he begins his awesome tasks.

When Jesus began his ministry, he delivered an inaugural address, too, most likely written without a team of consultants. And like those Washington speechwriters, Jesus also squirreled himself away for a while. Jesus always removed himself for a time of prayer before making his move.

After he was baptized by John at the River Jordan and received the mantle of "beloved Son" from his heavenly father, the Spirit drove him into the wilderness to think about what his life would be about. His experience there in the desert isn't so much a story of Jesus' external struggle with the devil as it is the story of his own internal struggle with himself, the temptation to use his gifts in wrong ways, to squander his privilege as God's beloved. Jesus spends forty difficult days in the wilderness, and emerges filled with clarity about his mission, ready to begin his ministry.

First item on the agenda: a trip back to his hometown, where, like a good Jewish boy, he goes to the synagogue in which he's grown up. To honor his return, the elders of his synagogue call him up front to read from the sacred texts. He chooses a passage from Isaiah, and in this "inaugural" speech, declares what's on his heart and what his life and ministry will be all about.

He unrolled the scroll and found the place where it was written:

> The Spirit of the Lord is upon me,
>   because he has anointed me
>   to bring good news to the poor.
> He has sent me to proclaim release to the captives
>   and recovery of sight to the blind,
>   to let the oppressed go free,
> to proclaim the year of the Lord's favor.

And he rolled up the scroll, gave it back to the attendant, and sat down. The eyes of all in the synagogue were fixed on him. Then he began to say to them, "Today this scripture has been fulfilled in your hearing." (Luke 4:7–21)

"Do you hear Isaiah's prophecy?" Jesus asked the people gathered in that small-town synagogue on that Sabbath day. "What you're seeing now is the beginning of the fulfillment of those prophetic dreams." Standing before the people he'd known since childhood, Jesus declared that he would preach good news to the poor, proclaim release to the captives, recover sight for the blind, and set free those who are oppressed. It was a memorable inaugural speech.

The rest of Luke's Gospel confirms that this is indeed what Jesus' ministry is about — touching lepers, embracing outcasts, honoring women and respecting children in ways unknown in that culture, loving the poor, refusing to stone the adulterous woman, including Gentiles in the kingdom, and telling stories of Good Samaritans and Prodigal Sons.

Jesus may have delivered that inaugural message a couple of thousand years ago, but the people who claim to be followers of Jesus must share in the ministry he proclaimed that day. Being

Christian isn't about building lovely churches and having beautiful music and a fine education program and youth group. It's not about right doctrine, and it's not even about being "good."

If you want to know what being a follower of Jesus is about, just check out his inaugural speech. It's about preaching good news to the poor, whether poor economically or poor in spirit. It's about releasing prisoners from all kinds of captivity. It's about restoring sight to people with all kinds of blindnesses. It's about working to set free those who are oppressed.

What Jesus' inauguration tells us — indeed, what Jesus tells us about himself — is that if you want to see God, this is where you need to go, this is what you need to do: preach the good news, release the prisoners, restore sight, bring freedom. You need to do these things with those who are most in need, those most desperate to hear of a God who loves them beyond imagining, with those who are most marginalized, most excluded, most irritating, most angry, most reprehensible, most unworthy, least acceptable by the world's standards.

I don't know about you, but this doesn't exactly fit my idea of good news. Frankly, I don't like hearing this, partly because I'm one of the privileged. I have more money than I need, I'm blessed beyond my wildest dreams, I live in a house ten times the size of most families in the world. I'm more educated than most people in the world, have never known hunger, have seen a good part of the world, and consume more than my fair share of what the poor of the world produce. I like my comfortable circumstances and my mostly predictable life.

And yet in his inaugural speech, Jesus asks me, "How are you going to spend the privilege you've been given? You know of God's love for you, and you draw enormous strength and comfort from that knowledge. But what good are you going to put that to? What risk are you going to take, what bold and daring thing are you going to do because of — and in service to — the Gospel? Because if you want to follow me, if you want to know me and be in relationship with me, this is where you've got to be: with the poor, with the prisoners, with the blind, the captive, the oppressed."

A church is more than a mutual admiration society. It exists for more than itself. If we are followers of Christ, we need to go where Christ is — which, as the Gospel tells us, is always with the poor, the dispossessed, and the marginalized — in New Hampshire or New York, in Manchester or Belfast, in El Salvador or West Africa. The question that faces every single person who takes the title of Christian is exactly the same question that Jesus faced in the wilderness after his baptism: "How will we spend the privilege that is ours? What risks will we take for the Gospel? What good will come to others from our knowing God's love for us?"

Will our participation in our own little part of the Body of Christ — our families, our parishes, our circles of friends — propel us into caring about the kind of ministry Jesus cared about? Or will we be content to stay safely warm and snug within our beautiful, well-cared-for walls? Will our "inreach" to one another be the security blanket we hold on to for comfort, or will our loving community give us the confidence and courage to engage in "outreach" to those who most need to hear that they too are loved by God?

And there are so many who don't know of God's love for them. Some live next door to you. Some sleep at night under bridges in our cities and towns. Some struggle with mental illness or addiction or AIDS in hospitals everywhere. Some scratch out a living in the dirt of a sub-Saharan African village. Who are the poor you can reach, and what is the good news they need and long to hear? Besides the obvious ones in your state or county, what kinds of prisons hold people captive, and what would set them free? Who are the blind, and by what are they blinded? What can you and God do to restore their sight? What fight are you willing to join in Jesus' name to free someone else from oppression?

If we are to see God, if we are to be doers of the Word and not just hearers only, we have to go where Jesus went. This is the bottom line: we cannot know God or follow Jesus without participating in the "pain of love and the work of justice." Every time we gather together as the body of Christ, it's inauguration day for the church. It's a time to celebrate the best news there is: that we are loved beyond our wildest imagining by the God of all creation. And it's an opportunity to ask ourselves this: From this day forward, what will our life and ministry be about? Just like Jesus, we too are the beloved of God, so how will we spend that privilege? What risks will we take because we are secure in that love? By virtue of Christ's death and resurrection the Spirit of the Lord is upon us just as surely as it was upon Jesus. And like Jesus, we too can — and must — go about the hard and holy work of fulfilling the scriptures in our own lives.

✳ 16 ✳

INFECTIOUS LOVE

Years ago I spoke at a youth ministries conference for a hundred or so teenagers. There was one very special kid at this event. He'd been a thalidomide baby; his mom had been prescribed that drug during her pregnancy, with serious consequences. As an older teenager, John stood about three and a half feet tall, with short, chubby legs that he sort of waddled around on, swinging from side to side to make headway. He had mostly stumps for arms, and I think one of them had a couple of fingers, or the beginnings of fingers on it. But he was a remarkable, bright, happy kid.

During the course of the conference I happened to be in the men's room, when in walks John, all three and a half feet of him, along with a strapping six-foot friend, both chatting about music, girlfriends, and other teenage interests. They casually sauntered over to one of the stalls — this was before we had handicapped-accessible bathrooms — and while they continued to chat, with no apparent discomfort at all, the six-foot guy put his foot up on the toilet, picked John up, and sat him on his knee. John relieved himself and zipped up, and all the time they're just chatting away as if this is how everybody went to the bathroom.

As one of the conference activities, we gave each of the small groups a Bible story to act out. Not surprisingly, one of them was the beloved parable of the Good Samaritan. Acting out the parable, one kid played the part of the priest, who walked by the injured man and did nothing to help. Another kid played the Levite, who likewise walked by without doing anything. And then in waddled John, on his short, stubby legs, who moseyed up to the injured man, reached down with his little stub of an arm, and brushed his cheek with the back of his two fingers, showing the kind of tenderness that must have been in the Samaritan's heart.

It's a scene that will be imprinted on my brain as long as I live. For me, the Good Samaritan will always be about three and a half feet tall and about as good a Samaritan as anybody could ever hope to be. But even though we call this story the parable of the Good Samaritan, the word "good" never appears anywhere in it. That reflects our tendency to rush to judgment about something. It reminds me of the cartoon where the dog is lying on his therapist's couch, saying, "It's always good dog or bad dog — why can't it just be judgment free?"

We always seem to rush to label things good and bad, and that's kind of what this story is about. All three of the main characters are good people. But two of them, the priest and the Levite, come off looking pretty bad. They're upstanding, religious people who actually take their faith seriously and know all the right answers to important questions. They can recite the creeds and the catechism and impressively long passages from scripture. They get it intellectually, theoretically, and perhaps even theologically, but maybe, Jesus seems to be saying, they don't get it in their hearts and their guts. Maybe it's not right belief or right thinking that gets to the heart of God, but actually doing God's will.

But let's cut the priest and the Levite a little slack. They had some very good reasons not to take care of this fellow on the side of the road. First of all, this road from Jericho to Jerusalem, which still exists today, was a seriously dangerous place, with robbers potentially lurking beyond every crooked bend. Slowing down for anything was a bad idea. After all, this guy in the ditch could have been a decoy, and the whole scenario could well have been a trap. It wasn't unusual for people to fake being hurt and ensnare unsuspecting travelers who might come to the rescue, robbing or even killing them.

Moreover, the priest and the Levite were good synagogue-goers. The priest would have been expected to go to Jerusalem, as every priest did, and serve for two weeks in the temple. And he knew, being a student of the law, that if he touched a dead body, he'd be ritually unclean, and it would take extensive purification rites before he'd be allowed to perform the service he was scheduled to give. So why would he risk touching this comatose traveler, only to find that he was dead, and in the process risk defiling himself and delaying his service in the temple? Yes, the priest and the Levite were "good" people.

And then along comes the Samaritan. Let's remember that he is a character in the Gospel of Luke, an account written by an outsider for other outsiders. Luke is someone who has traditionally been excluded from "God's chosen people," writing for other Gentiles. He understands that his portrayal of Jesus would be a challenge for the early church to hear, embroiled as it was over the inclusion of Gentiles. He probably knew that some of his stories of Jesus would turn the whole world upside down. So, true to form, it's the Samaritan — from that race of people despised and shunned by the Jews — who actually does the will of God. The priest and the Levite, who perhaps know the will of God, can't quite bring themselves to do it. Yet the marginalized Samaritan finds it in his heart to reach out.

Don't forget the setting and context of this story: a bright young lawyer has asked Jesus, "What must we do to gain eternal life?" When Jesus counters with a question of his own — What does the Bible say? — the lawyer gets it right. "To love God with all your heart, soul, mind, and strength. And to love your neighbor as yourself." And Jesus says, "A-plus, very good," but he pushes the envelope: "Who exactly *is* your neighbor?" he demands. That one seems to stump the lawyer, so Jesus tells this story of the Good Samaritan to show what love of God looks like detached from love of neighbor. The lawyer got the "love of

God" part; he understood that. But he didn't quite connect that to the love of neighbor, which is really at the heart of the Gospel.

The Christian life, after all, isn't just about life after death. It's also about life *before* death. Whatever God does for us after death, God will take care of. But what we do with life before death is up to us. And that's the real reward of Christianity. Not some pie-in-the-sky prize, but rather a blessing to us in *this* life. It's not an accident that in our confession, and in the absolution that follows, we don't say, "and may God *bring* you to everlasting life," but rather "may God *keep* you in everlasting life." Our reward starts now if we are awake, if we understand that in the doing of God's will, we already participate in everlasting life. It's right action — not right belief, not right thinking — that gets us to the heart of God.

A while back, in the only conversation I've ever had with the Archbishop of Canterbury, he explained to me that what the Episcopal Church should have done prior to electing and consecrating me bishop was to have figured out these hot-button issues theologically and intellectually and ecclesiologically. We should've come to a common mind, and then passed canons, and consented to my episcopacy only after doing our homework. But I responded, with respect, that all the great steps toward justice the church has taken have been the result of our somehow finding the courage to do the right thing and then thinking it through later — not the other way around.

Think about it. If we'd waited, for instance, in the United States for everyone to agree about civil rights, there might still be separate drinking fountains for blacks and whites. If we'd waited until women were valued as full and equal members of society and the human race, the great strides toward women's equality still wouldn't have happened. Does anyone think that if the so-called Philadelphia 11 hadn't been "irregularly" ordained in 1974, we'd have proceeded to ordaining women canonically two years later? Who knows when it would have happened? And in the Church of England, has anything been really gained from allowing "flying bishops"[1] to have jurisdiction in those places still resistant to the acceptance of women in the life and leadership of the church? "Right" and careful thinking led the priest and the Levite to ignore the hurting man on the side of the road, and I suspect the same is true for us. Sometimes our careful thinking leads us away from doing the will of God. Maybe the sneaker commercial gets it right when it challenges us to "Just do it."

In the parable, the light bulb is starting to switch on over the lawyer's head. "So what must I do, what must I do?" he demands. And Jesus tells the story of the Good Samaritan, and the answer seems to be, love in a way that actually costs you something: costs you time, costs you money, costs you focus, costs you convenience. To gain eternal life, you need to experience *that* kind of love for your neighbor.

There was a young seminarian who worked one summer with an old priest at a homeless shelter where they had a noontime feeding program. On this particular day, there was an unusually large number of people who came to be fed. The priest and the seminarian were just exhausted — it was nearly three o'clock before the last person left. The priest asked the seminarian to close the front door and shut down for the day. Just as this young seminarian got to the door, thinking that this long and difficult day was about to be over, he saw yet one more homeless man making his way up the walk. In his exhausted state, thinking he had no energy left, nothing left to give, he exclaimed, "Jesus Christ!"

And the old priest remarked, "It just might be."

Love that costs, even when we think we're depleted, is the love of neighbor Jesus calls us to. Have you ever thrown away an old tube of toothpaste and then gone to the closet to discover that

---

1. "Flying bishops": the informal term used to describe bishops in the English church opposed to the ordination of women and who are allowed to minister outside their geographically defined dioceses to congregations who share their anti-women's ordination views.

you forgot to buy another one? Then you reach into the trash can, and retrieve the old tube and discover that you can always squeeze out just enough for one more time? Our life with God is exactly like that. There's always enough "toothpaste in the tube" to help one more person. Just when we think there's nothing left to give, if we make the simplest effort, God provides manna in the desert — maybe just enough for that day, but it's enough. God gives us what we need to respond in the way the Good Samaritan responded. That's the real miracle of life in God.

Love that costs means that we must get our hands dirty and really *do* the work of ministry, not just give a nod to it. Episcopal author and activist Louie Crew has pointed out the only real mistake made in the catechism in the Book of Common Prayer (p. 847). The catechism's question is, "What response did God require from the chosen people?" The prayer book answer — it's supposed to be a quote from Micah the Prophet — reads: "to love justice, to do mercy, and to walk humbly with their God."

Well, that would all be very nice except that's not what Micah said! What Micah really said: "to do justice, to love mercy, and to walk humbly with our God" (Mic. 6:8). What a telling comment on human nature that such a transposition got made in the text, because, after all, it's a lot easier to love justice than to *do* justice! We love to talk about justice, convene committees about justice, plan for justice, but the thing that is hardest is *doing* justice. What Jesus teaches in the story of the Good Samaritan is that it's not enough to be good. It's not enough to know the creeds and say you believe all the things that you're supposed to believe. It's not even enough just to love God. What counts is how love of God translates into love of neighbor. What counts is what you do.

Our baptismal covenant, which is as close to a purpose statement as we have in the Episcopal Church, contains all action verbs. The baptismal covenant is not about which doctrines you ascribe to, but about loving and serving one another. It's about respecting the dignity of every human being. It's about repenting and coming back to God. It's all about doing. What we see in the story of the Good Samaritan is the danger of loving God in our heads and separating that from loving our neighbors with our actions.

The real challenge of this story is whether or not we want to be admirers of Jesus or disciples of Jesus. It's easy to admire Jesus, to think he was a nifty guy with wonderful, worthy ideas. Following Jesus, being his disciple, is a whole lot harder. Doing the work of ministry and doing justice — getting into Gospel trouble — is what we are meant to do. That's what makes disciples out of us.

Jesus, of course, got into lots of trouble. The Romans killed lots of people, but they saved crucifixion for a very specific kind of criminal: the one who challenged the powers that be, who took on the government, who threatened the Pax Romana with notions of turning the world upside down — like Jesus did. And they didn't put them all high and lifted up, like in a movie. Crosses were actually quite low to the ground, so that as people died and began to rot away, the dogs could eat their flesh and there'd be almost nothing left to bury. The Romans wanted to make a real example of anyone who challenged Rome.

It's an indictment of each of us that we can wear a cross around our necks, hang it on our walls, and even display it on church steeples, and it doesn't threaten anybody. When we wear a cross, it ought to scare people to death — at least those powers-that-be that continue to prey on the vulnerable. The more powerful they are, the more it ought to scare them. If we were making the kind of trouble Jesus did, we would be followed around by the FBI or Scotland Yard. When we put on the cross of Christ, we're saying that it's not just religion that we are about. We are about changing the world, as Jesus changed it. We are about loving the people that Jesus loved: those on the margins. That doesn't mean sitting in a committee and talking about loving those people, but actually loving them, and doing the hard work of justice. Will we be admirers of Jesus, or will we be disciples?

Christianity has become too tame, too predictable, too proper. Instead of going to church to be energized for mission, ministry, and justice, all too often we go for an "inoculation" instead.

Think about the way inoculation works. You don't want to get chicken pox, so you go to the doctor, who gives you just enough chicken pox to make your body form antibodies to it. So you never get a full-blown case of chicken pox. Could it be that we actually go to church for such an inoculation? God help us if we go to church on Sunday mornings just to get enough religion to keep us from having a full-blown case. If we took to heart what we read in scripture and hear in church, we would set about changing our own lives and seeking to transform the world. A "full-blown case" of Christianity would result in befriending the oppressed, working for justice, and offering ourselves sacrificially in God's plan for the salvation of the world. Inoculated from such a serious case of Christianity, most of us settle for a watered-down version of what Jesus taught the young lawyer about whose neighbor he was.

After all, it's really easy for us to go to church, and it feels so good. You see people you know, and the music's great, and the preaching is good, and it's a pretty good way to spend an hour or so. But if we leave church and don't do anything any differently, then church is nothing but a religious theme park.

We have to be out there doing the work that God has given us to do, or else our faith is just self-serving. It's very hard work. When Jesus says take up your cross and follow me, he means it's going to be tough. It means taking risks; it means loving in a way that costs. But the miracle is that when we do that and we face that trouble, we come to know the very God who is at the center of all that is. It's the only way we get to know God.

✻ 17 ✻

RELIGION AND POLITICS

Ask almost anybody. The conventional wisdom is that religion and politics don't mix. My response is probably a little unconventional: I say that for people of faith, religion and politics *must* mix. But not in the way that we've seen from the Religious Right.

The United States was founded by people escaping theocracies in Europe, and even today we're seeing the horrifying results of theocracies in other parts of the world. The last thing we need is a Christian theocracy in America, where the tenets of one brand of Christianity are imposed on the citizenry. When people of faith mix religion and politics, the goal should be to allow our Christian beliefs and values to inform our personal politics and our political decisions without foisting them on others.

Here's the way I look at the mix: it really doesn't matter which party or which candidate anyone chooses to support — that's always a very personal decision. But it's crucial to contemplate the values we hold as Christians before we come to that decision, making sure that the candidate we support holds those values too. We dwell of course in the realm of reality, and no candidate is perfect or even close to it — humankind and politics being what they are. There's no candidate any of us will always agree with, no party that perfectly embodies our dearly held values. But politics is the art of the possible, and we must make choices among those candidates presented to us.

The United States — and all Western democracies — stands at the threshold of an uncertain future. But instead of focusing on the important issues, we seem to be polarized and paralyzed:

border security and immigration; traditional families and gay marriage; the thirst for petroleum and the future of the planet. Everybody — and every cause — seems to be pitted against everybody else. Yet we are desperate for a way out of the polarizing atmosphere within which we try to have civil discourse about the nation — indeed about the world. We desperately need to look at the future, not the future of one party or another, not the candidacy of one politician or another, not even the fate of one country or another. We need to look at the future of all nations, because we are all in this together.

As Christians, we need to support public servants who have a vision for reconciliation rather than further polarization and division. It doesn't take much to see that reconciliation is a Christian value. Just look at the ministry of Jesus. The Gospel is a pretty clear sign that we must end the demonization of our enemies, whether they're members or candidates of the "other" party, or our "enemies" around the world. Our Christian faith tells us that it's time to worry less about narrowly winning a vote and more about achieving a consensus on how our country and our world must move and act, both at home and among the family of nations.

As individual Christians and citizens of democracies, of course, we're free to mix religion and politics. For members of the clergy and representatives of religious institutions, it's another story. In the United States, a person of faith can say anything he or she wants to say as a citizen; free speech is a hugely important value in a democracy. For members of the clergy, it's a little dicey. We can say whatever we want to, as long as it's not from a pulpit, not at a church meeting or gathering, not in a church publication, and as long as we're not speaking, or insinuating that we're speaking, for our congregation or our institution.

When I endorsed a candidate for the U.S. presidential primary in 2007, I spoke only as a private citizen; I spoke for no one but myself. When I endorsed that candidate, in neither my own comments nor in the questions put to me by the press, were the words "Episcopal" or "Diocese of New Hampshire" ever used.

Each of us needs to take the Gospel into account and then speak the Gospel for ourselves, in our own words, in our elections for president and prime minister and school board representative. All religious people ought to take stock of the values they hold, find a candidate — of whatever party — who best embodies those values, and then work for that candidate and become a part of important civil discourse. You could argue convincingly that in some ways, because of my public role, I will never again be just a "private citizen." Because of that, my remarks and choices as a private citizen are more likely to be reported than the comments of others. But I don't believe that such a circumstance means that I should keep silent.

The issues that face us as citizens are moral in nature, and morality is our purview as people who call themselves Christian. Think of the questions that face us: Should we intervene in the genocide going on in Darfur? What should we do about the ever-widening gap between rich and poor all around the world? What is the most humane way to extricate ourselves from Iraq (not to mention the question of whether or not it was moral to preemptively attack in the first place)? How do we adequately protect ourselves from the threat of terrorism without sacrificing our civil rights, or our souls? How can the United States of America, the richest nation on earth, not provide health-care coverage to the 45 million people who currently have none? How can we use up more of the earth's resources than any other nation, relative to our population, and then balk at doing our part to be responsible stewards of the environment? Are these not moral questions as well as political ones?

I believe all Christians should get involved in politics. Just as "liturgy" is the worshipful work of the people, so is "politics" the work of the *polis,* the people, the body politic. As people in the world, Christians must assume their rightful role in helping shape the choices we make as a nation, as citizens of the world. For me, especially in New Hampshire, with its important role in the American presidential primary process, this includes getting involved in politics.

Priests, imams, ministers, and rabbis can always broadcast their general and unspecific hope that everyone should take their civic duty seriously and get involved, but for the most part, nobody pays very much attention to that amorphous direction. But when religious people — those who are known in their communities as people of faith and those who represent congregations — speak out on specific issues, their words are likely to spark a lively conversation. The conversation won't be about a particular candidate or cause, but about our call as Christians to affect the world in which we live. We'll disagree, of course, on which candidates and approaches best speak to those issues; there's nothing wrong or fearful about that. We'll prefer different economic and diplomatic strategies, and the candidates who propose them; nothing wrong with that, either. And then, as good citizens, we'll support and respect the will of the majority. That is what is great — even miraculous — about democracy. But let's not abdicate the role of making the connections between our faith and our politics to those on the Religious Right.

It's vital that religious people keep the lines of communication open as they search for the candidate whose policies seem best to reflect real Christian values. It's vital that we recognize that the major issues that affect us in the United States, the United Kingdom, Canada, and all across the globe are moral issues as well as political issues. It's vital that we do all we can to bring our faith to the public debate, not in an attempt to impose our beliefs on others, but to witness to the fact that our faith informs our worldly choices. For Christians, religion and politics *must* mix.

Part Five

THE COMPASS ROSE

Charting the Course
of the Anglican Communion

O God the Father of our Lord Jesus Christ, our only Savior,
the Prince of Peace: Give us grace seriously to lay to heart
the great dangers we are in by our unhappy divisions; take
away all hatred and prejudice, and whatever else may hinder
us from godly union and concord; that, as there is but one
Body and one Spirit, one hope of our calling, one Lord, one
Faith, one Baptism, one God and Father of us all, so we
may be all of one heart and one soul, united in one holy
bond of truth and peace, of faith and charity, and may with
one mind and one mouth glorify you; through Jesus Christ
our Lord. Amen.

— Prayer for the Unity of the Church,
The Book of Common Prayer, p. 818

B Y ANY STANDARD, the Anglican Communion is in crisis.
Some say the election of a gay bishop has caused that crisis.
But the crisis goes much deeper, reaches much more broadly. It
has to do with scripture and authority, with shifting power and
changing priorities, with globalization and lack of resources, with

our differing understandings of ordination and the role of bishops. It's actually been a long time coming, and it's not apt to be solved anytime soon.

The Anglican Communion is a blessing, a gift from God. While it may look like our own creation, it is actually the resulting gift of our brotherhood and sisterhood in Christ that comes from baptism. We must cling to one another while we disagree about issues of the day, because we are indissolubly bound in Christ, commonly nourished on Christ's Body and Blood, and bound for eternal life in God's kingdom. Do we have the will to *be* the family God wills us to be?

* 18 *

BLESSED MINORITY REPORT

On a sabbatical trip to several nations on the Pacific Rim, I was invited to meet with the Blessed Minority Christian Fellowship in Hong Kong. It's a gathering of a hundred or so gay and lesbian Christians in their twenties. It's not like other churches: you can't just show up at the door on a Sunday morning. To get in, you need to know a person who's already in the fellowship, or be put in touch with them by someone the community knows and trusts. After you make your request, you get an invitation to meet one member of the community on a certain street corner or at a particular phone booth, and from there, if you pass muster, you'll be led to the secret meeting place of the fellowship. It sounds very cloak-and-dagger, but it's very serious business. That's because to be openly gay or lesbian in Hong Kong is dangerous. It comes with great risk, and serious consequences.

Many of these young people worship at their own churches on Sunday morning, but they don't bring their entire selves to those gatherings. In their "regular churches," they cannot speak of the person God made them to be and called good. In their "regular churches," where gay and lesbian people — people like them — are still called an abomination, these young people have no hope of putting their sexuality and their spirituality together. And so on Sunday afternoons they come to a secret place to sing songs of praise and to worship the God who redeemed them and loves them exactly as they are.

I was invited to that secret place, and when I arrived, I couldn't help thinking about the early Christian communities that met in the catacombs of Rome, tiny gatherings of people who risked life and limb to worship God as revealed in Jesus Christ. So on fire with the Gospel message were they that they refused to let the supremely powerful and extremely hostile Roman Empire extinguish the light of Christ that shone in them. And though this modern-day little "underground" gathering took place on the twenty-fifth floor of a Hong Kong highrise, it too was a catacomb of sorts. And the courage and hope of this gathering of the faithful, who refused to deny the Light of Christ within them, matched the courage and valor of any first-century Christian. Only this time, the powerful and hostile empire is not only the government, but the church itself. Not only are there consequences to be paid for being openly gay as a citizen; there are spiritual consequences to be paid for being gay and Christian in the church, an institution that still, for the most part, considers them an abomination.

The oppression these gay and lesbian Christians face comes in a lot of different packages. If they pursue a "don't ask, don't tell" strategy, they pay an emotional price for hiding their true selves. And if they come out, they face more serious consequences: being ostracized by their Christian community and singled out for condemnation. These young Christians, who happen to be gay and lesbian, are damned if they do and damned if they don't. They face political and social oppression from society and spiritual oppression from fellow Christians. Alienation from one's brothers and sisters in Christ, even and especially during the act of worship, is a particularly painful consequence of this "don't ask, don't tell" reality. The message they hear from the church is loud and clear: it's bad enough that you are who you are; don't compound your sin by claiming God's blessing on you and your kind.

Here's the part that's astonishing and even humbling. Every single one of these "kids," no matter what Christian denomination they belong to, is following our debate in America and in the Anglican Communion. They know about my election and the stir it has caused. They follow everything we do and say. They somehow perceive — and I wonder if they're right — that their own liberation is tied to ours.

They wanted to thank me, they wanted to touch me, they wanted to tell me their stories. They asked questions and listened intently as my words were translated into Chinese for the non-English speakers. They wanted their pictures taken with me — not because of me, but because I was the outward and visible link to the church that is leading the way to a new kind of inclusive church. A photograph with the Bishop of New Hampshire, with his arm around them, tacked up on a bulletin board in their room, is a physical and symbolic reminder that there is hope for them and for their church.

When the service was over, I looked for the young man who had led the spirited music, with his fine voice and affable demeanor, but he seemed to have disappeared right after my talk. Someone pointed to a side alcove, where I found him crying. I asked if he was all right. He replied that not for a very long time had he had such a palpable and powerful experience of the Holy Spirit. So I just held this young man while he wept.

I told the group that I would always hold them close to my heart, that I would tell their story wherever I went, and that I would never forget them. I know that whenever I am feeling discouraged or impatient or angry, I will remember them and renew my own resolve. And I now know, in a deeper way than ever before, that the good news I preached to them on that Sunday afternoon in Hong Kong is the same good news for me and for all of us: that God says to each of us the words God said to the Son at his baptism, "You are my beloved child. In you I am well pleased." Let our tears of thanksgiving flow. And let the church say "Amen."

In that little apartment on the twenty-fifth floor of a Hong Kong highrise I learned again that we're all in this together. Everything we do in our congregations, our workplaces, and our families — all of it has a ripple effect. And the actions we take in the Episcopal Church have ramifications around the world for our brothers and sisters in Christ. Sometimes, we are told, those ramifications are negative and divisive. But sometimes, especially to the ears of the discounted, despised and marginalized, those ramifications are breathtakingly holy, bringing life and hope to those whom Christ came to serve.

✽ 19 ✽

WHAT ARE THEY AFRAID OF?

We commit ourselves to listen to the experience of homo-
sexual persons and we wish to assure them that they are
loved by God and that all baptised, believing and faithful
persons, regardless of sexual orientation, are full members
of the Body of Christ.
— 1998 Lambeth Conference of Bishops,
Resolution 1.10 (c)

Notes from the far reaches of the Anglican Communion, during
my November 2007 sabbatical trip to the Pacific Rim:

◆ I travel some seventeen thousand miles to meet with the primate of a remote province of the Anglican Communion. After
I've spent some wonderful time in his dioceses, he declines to
meet with me after all, though I am staying less than three
hundred yards from his office. "It is," I am told, "just too
dangerous locally for him to do so."

◆ During a private meeting with another primate, every mention
of every difficult subject is politely ignored. The primate simply
acts as if I've never spoken the words he prefers not to hear.
He is pleasant and hospitable, but steadfastly ignores any attempts to talk about the issues that divide us. Not once does
he ask, "How is life in your diocese?" Though I am genuinely
interested in life and ministry in his diocese and province, he
doesn't seem to want to know about life and ministry in New
Hampshire.

◆ The editor of an Australian church publication hears that I'll be visiting Australia and calls the primate. He inquires whether the archbishop and I have a meeting scheduled (we don't), and — if I were to request one (I had no plans to do so) — would he meet with me (he said he'd be willing to do as part of the Lambeth listening process). The editor brings this non-story about a non-event to a leading conservative group and seeks a comment. The conservative leader obliges. He proclaims that such a meeting would constitute an inappropriately "close alliance" of the primate with one side of a debate going on in the Communion. All these machinations to block a conversation that was never scheduled or sought in the first place!

◆ A wonderful new bishop, who had previously given me permission to accept an invitation to speak in one of his parishes, calls and asks me to delay my visit by a year. The bishop confides that the conservatives in his diocese have launched a campaign against him because of his decision to allow my visit. So rather than allowing me to speak with his people, he proposes that two *other* bishops, one liberal and one conservative, come and talk *about* gay people first. I've been very clear that I'd never do anything in his diocese without his express permission, and I honor his wishes.

Over a period of four weeks, I traveled thirty thousand miles to a number of countries to hear the stories of other Anglicans and to share my own story. Listening to one another, after all, is something we Anglicans are deeply committed to. At least on paper.

But what I found, to my dismay, was that in many places, there isn't a whole lot of listening going on. There's been a lot of lip service paid to two-way listening between those who disagree about the nature and morality of homosexuality. I couldn't agree more that two-way, mutual listening is key to our overall relationships in the Communion. But the specific call from the Lambeth Conferences has been for listening to the stories of gay and lesbian members of the church, and that is happening in too few places across the Communion.

Why not? I think it's because of fear. But what exactly are people afraid of? What's the worst that could happen if a gay or lesbian person were to be known to have sat down with a primate? He could be "accused" of complying with the recommendations of the Windsor Report and the last three Lambeth Conferences — which seems like a very good thing. Could an archbishop's reputation for doctrinal purity and moral uprightness be jeopardized by a conversation with gay Anglicans? Presumably not, if the archbishop continued his traditional attitudes toward homosexuality. There's nothing in the nature of listening that says the hearer must change his mind. Consider the example of Jesus himself. On numerous occasions, he conversed and even dined with notorious sinners, and while it brought him criticism from some quarters, we certainly don't accuse him of being "soft on sin." A display of such Christlike hospitality in listening to all voices in the Communion should only increase the archbishop's moral authority.

Would merely associating with one of the "sides" in the heated debates that are raging about homosexuality necessarily impede the primate's efforts to pastor *all* "sides"? Not if the pastor remained open and sensitive to all opinions, willing to be in conversation with any and all. Simply meeting with those who hold a different view doesn't signal capitulation to that view. Even if someone is dead wrong on this issue — morally, spiritually, and biblically — that person is still worthy of his bishop's pastoral care.

I wonder if the real fear behind all this anxiety could be summed up with this question: "What if we're wrong after all?" My speech in a conservative diocese can be scary to conservatives only because my witness might be compelling. Surely I'm not smart enough or clever enough to undo a lifetime of "orthodox" teaching in a one-hour talk and twenty minutes of questions-and-answers. Surely if my arguments are so flawed, both morally and biblically, my listeners will see through them. And even if they don't, there will be plenty of conservatives on hand to raise objections, ask questions, and point out the errors of my ways. Maybe the real fear in allowing people to listen to me is that I *might not* appear crazy, immoral, illogical, or faithless.

And if that's the case, what people are really fearful of is: (1) that faithful, believing Anglicans who happen to be gay or lesbian will look and act and sound like most other Anglicans; (2) that the arguments for changing our traditional understanding of homosexuality will make sense — ethically, biblically, scientifically, and spiritually; and (3) that even if we don't agree about the issue of homosexuality, that won't necessarily be a good reason to split our beloved church apart in rancorous debate and costly litigation.

In the Book of Acts, the Synagogue council in Jerusalem seeks to have Peter and the other disciples silenced. The Council is afraid of what might happen if the people hear the disciples' preaching — after all, some might actually believe them. But the wise rabbi Gamaliel offers good counsel to his leaders: if this is not of God, it will soon wither away, and we needn't worry about it. But if it *is* of God, then do we really want to be against it? Let the disciples of Jesus speak, the rabbi proposes. Trust the people to find the truth, and don't get in the way of the Spirit (see Acts 5:21–42).

But in the wider Anglican Communion today, when it comes to the stories and lives of gay men and lesbians, there is virtually *no* listening going on. Not really. Here and there people who have talked about these issues for thirty years continue to do so, but some of them are simply tired of reworking the same ground and know there are more important things to tend to. In some parts

of the Communion, where disease, starvation, and economic un-
derdevelopment are the pressing issues of existence, arguments
about sexuality take a back seat altogether, as they should. And
in dioceses and provinces around the globe headed by very conservative leadership, there are no safe places for anyone to talk
openly about these issues without fear of negative consequences,
and gay or lesbian people would have to be crazy and virtually
suicidal to come forward to tell their own story. Even in moder-
ate dioceses, there is an attempt, either unconscious or carefully
planned, to polarize the situation and to forestall any real listening by threatening bishops and budgets with dire consequences if
conversation is allowed to happen.

Fear is a terrible thing. It does terrible things to people and
to institutions. Perhaps that's why the admonition to "fear not"
and "be not afraid" appear so often in scripture. Jesus' whole
life is framed by it: from the "Fear not, for behold I bring you
good tidings of great joy" at his birth, to his calming "do not be
afraid" words of comfort at every resurrection appearance. One
of the meanings, one of the payoffs, of the Gospel is the banishing
of fear from our lives. It has been argued that the opposite of faith
is not doubt or unbelief, but fear.

More than twenty years ago, when my wife and I made the
decision to end our marriage, I was approached by an older priest
in the diocese who was troubled about my coming out. For the
next two decades, we held on to each other while we discussed
the issues of homosexuality and faith, though he steadfastly held
to his belief that homosexuality was incompatible with scripture
and ordination.

He was part of a committee on which I sat, and he refused to
attend a dinner at my house at the end of the committee's work. I
wrote to him that rather than being afraid of what he might see,
perhaps his refusal to attend was more a fear of what he would
not see. No obscene pictures on the walls, no "flaunting" of some

stereotypical "lifestyle," nothing to which he would object. I wondered if he was afraid that he'd see a Christian household and family, no better and no worse than any other household trying to live out the best of Christian values.

Later, at a clergy conference, he came to me in tears and said, "I'm not sure what to believe anymore. For my whole ministry, I've done and believed as the church has instructed me, yet I'm confused and in turmoil. *You,* on the other hand, having gone against the church's teaching, seem to be happy and at peace! What gives?" We continued to talk to each other, and in our talking, we continued to *love* each other. During the course of that conference, the bishop was called away, and it fell to me, as Canon to the Ordinary, to celebrate the Eucharist at the end of the gathering.

As I was saying the words of consecration, it occurred to me that this wonderful, faithful priest would soon have to present himself to me to receive the Body of Christ, and I knew he must be experiencing conflicting emotions because of that. But sure enough, there he was, waiting his turn to receive communion from my hands. When I placed the bread in his outstretched hands and said, "The Body of Christ, the bread of heaven," we both burst into tears. In that moment, I knew that somehow, it was going to be all right.

That priest and elder of our church later went on to propose changing the name of our mid-winter clergy and spouses conference to the "clergy and partners" conference. He was the first to welcome my partner, Mark, to that event. He even sat and talked to him about what it meant to be there, and he listened to Mark's reply. Later, he would hire as his assistant the first openly gay man to be ordained to the priesthood in this diocese.

After his retirement, this humble man attended a lunch Mark and I gave for retired clergy. By this time, he was suffering severely from Parkinson's disease and was "eating" through a feeding tube in his stomach. But he wanted to be there. After I became bishop,

Mark and I renovated part of our house so that we'd be able to entertain larger groups from the diocese. As part of that renovation, we made our downstairs handicapped-accessible, installing a lift in our garage up to the first-floor. After using the lift, with his walker, this priest asked, "Did you put that lift in for someone in your family, or did you do it for people like me?" When I indicated the latter, he began to cry. If no one else ever used that lift, it had paid for itself that day.

It was my honor and privilege, as his bishop, to preside at his funeral and celebratory Eucharist. There are all sorts of courage, but I will always think that his courage stands out over the rest. Risking life and limb is easy, compared to risk changing one's mind. His change of heart came about because he was a man of prayer. Despite everything he'd been taught, he kept his heart open to God's leading. His fear of change was overcome by his desire to do God's will, to hear God's voice, and to follow wherever God might lead. His love of me, as a human being and a child of God, is one of the greatest gifts I have ever received.

Fear is a terrible thing. And there is a lot of it in the Anglican Communion right now. It is the opposite of faith. The truth is, the near absence of any real "listening process" is an absence of faith and a capitulation to fear, not a defense of doctrinal purity. Thanks be to God, "perfect love casts out fear" (1 John 4:18).

✳ 20 ✳

RECONCILIATION:
THE TOUGHEST LOVE

The Anglican Communion is in turmoil. Headlines in newspapers around the world herald disagreement and conflict, even schism. Some threaten to leave over perceived differences; others risk being expelled by their longtime brother and sister Anglicans around the world because of disagreements with the majority over particular issues.

Yet according to scripture, we are given the ministry of reconciliation — with God and with one another. How are we to understand that ministry in a worldwide church torn apart by issues of human sexuality, polity, and the meaning of brotherhood and sisterhood in the Body of Christ?

And where are we to turn for help in understanding reconciliation? The world is crawling with experts, on almost any topic you can imagine, from how to invest in real estate to how to become a public speaker, from cooking the perfect soufflé to getting a perfect score on university entrance exams. But on the topic of reconciliation in the Anglican Communion (or elsewhere, for that matter), there are simply no experts. There certainly do not appear to be any easy answers.

When it comes to what I believe about reconciliation, I'm enormously indebted to a recent book by Miguel De La Torre called *Liberating Jonah: Forming an Ethics of Reconciliation*.[1]

---

1. Miguel A. De La Torre, *Liberating Jonah: Forming an Ethics of Reconciliation* (Maryknoll, N.Y.: Orbis Books, 2007).

The author is associate professor of ethics and director of the Justice and Peace Institute at Iliff School of Theology, a United Methodist institution in Denver, Colorado. He uses the topic of race to talk about the relationship between empire and the marginalized, between the oppressors and the oppressed. Both the oppressors and the oppressed, he says, need each other for the salvation of both. And, he notes — and this is important — reconciliation isn't the same as peace, and it's much more than forgiveness or the mere absence of conflict.

As a matter of fact, De La Torre insists, the process of reconciliation has conflict built right into it. Indeed, the alternative worldview brought from the margins by the oppressed to the oppressors is always a challenge to the powers-that-be. So isn't it amazing that the church finds conflict so surprising within its ranks? If it weren't for conflict, we wouldn't have most of the New Testament. Paul didn't write all those letters to the Christians in Corinth and Rome and Galatia to pat them on the back and tell them to keep up the good work. He wrote those letters to try to keep all those newly minted Christians from tearing each other apart with one fight or another. So it's odd that two thousand years later we're surprised and distressed that we're still not exactly getting along. But why should Christians be so intimidated and fearful over conflict?

Think about what we hear over and over again, in the Hebrew and Christian scriptures, from the mouths of angels and prophets and from Jesus himself: "Be not afraid." Jesus' life is bookended with that advice: At his birth, shepherds in their fields are told, "Fear not. For behold, I bring you good tidings of great joy." And at the end of his life on earth, in every single one of his resurrection appearances, the first words Jesus utters are "Don't be afraid, don't be afraid." That was good advice then, and it's good advice now, in the midst of the current conflict in the Anglican Communion. We need not be afraid of conflict. It's going to be hard, and we usually won't know if what we're doing is right. But we need not be afraid.

The scriptures also have a lot to say about love. And since we're talking about reconciliation, it's important to say that love means way more than being nice. In Christendom, there's probably nobody better at being nice than Anglicans. But the kind of love the scriptures talk about has more to do with loving justice, and the hard work of doing justice rarely involves being nice.

That means that it's not enough for us to gather on Sunday morning and say how much we love and admire Jesus: "Wasn't he a great guy? Didn't he say some really remarkable things? Aren't we great to love him too?" But being disciples requires far more risky behavior and demands far more courage than being merely admirers. In the Anglican Communion, our greatest danger just might be that we've become Jesus' admirers rather than Jesus' disciples.

Discipleship is a difficult and complicated calling. We live out our discipleship in what we do and what we don't do, in what we say and what we don't say. Discipleship is more than "do no harm," more than being careful not to say or do anything hurtful. Discipleship is more proactive, more willing to take risks, more involved in the actual dismantling and undoing of injustice.

Discipleship demands action — not just loving justice, but doing justice. Charity is good as far as it goes; but the Gospel demands that we go beyond charity and do the work of justice. As the old saying goes, "It's not enough to pull the drowning victims from the stream — that's charity. We must walk upstream and stop whoever is throwing them in — that's justice."

The current debates over human sexuality in the Anglican Communion have implications for both charity and justice. On the one hand, kindly and sympathetic treatment of members of our church who are gay, lesbian, bisexual, or transgendered would be a wonderful thing. It certainly beats disdain, condemnation, and hatred. But beyond changing those negative feelings, we need to ask the justice questions involved in this debate.

Our struggles now in the Episcopal Church are similar to those in the 1960s, when the church was trying to decide whether or not to get actively involved in the civil rights movement. At that time, a lot of people thought we should steer clear of the issue of civil rights for people of color. Many threatened to leave if we got involved — and to take their membership and their pledges with them. Many in the church, bishops and rectors and vestry members and people in the pews, argued against our activism by saying that we needed to be pastoral to those people who were in a different place regarding our treatment of other races. We could, it was argued, effect more change by using a "go-slow," pastoral approach to those who resisted full participation of black people in the society and in the church.

At some point, though, we turned a corner. We decided to do the right thing, supporting African Americans in their struggles for equal rights, and then dealing as pastorally as we could with those who didn't understand, didn't agree, or didn't stay. The Episcopal Church paid a price for that action. Some did leave, taking their substantial money with them. Some clergy were hounded out of their pulpits for suggesting that the Gospel commanded such a commitment to the human dignity of all. Some congregations paid the price for their activism; some merely founded private schools where their children could be taught in an all-white environment.

We are at a similar moment today with respect to the issue of full inclusion of gay and lesbian people in the life and leadership of the church, except that we have not yet turned that crucial corner. Today, we are still concerned with being pastoral to those who oppose any acceptance of the gay and lesbian members of the church, be they laity or clergy. Many are intimidated by conservative threats to leave the Episcopal Church. We have not yet turned the corner in our understanding of this as a justice issue.

As a church, we still haven't decided to do the right thing, and then deal as pastorally as we can with those who do not understand or who disagree. Today — as in the 1960s with the issue of race — we desperately need to understand that the way we treat our gay, lesbian, bisexual, and transgender brothers and sisters in Christ is a matter of justice. Only then will we be able to do the right thing. Only then will we be emboldened not only to love justice, but to *do* justice.

How do we move from justice to reconciliation? If the work of justice brings tension, challenge, and conflict, how do we move toward reconciliation? What would the work of reconciliation look like? Back to De La Torre's discussion of Jonah.

Remember the Old Testament story of Jonah and the whale? That's as good a place as any for us to mine the guts of reconciliation. Most of us think the story is just about a guy being swallowed by a big fish, but it's really about Jonah's call from God to speak the truth and be an agent of reconciliation in the midst of a harsh and conflicted world. Jonah, of course, has been used for a long time as an example of how we enlightened Christians ought to take the Gospel to the heathen — to those pagans, usually in Africa, Asia, or Latin America, who don't know the light of Christ and need us to tell them about it. Jonah has long been understood as the reluctant evangelist.

But in *Liberating Jonah,* De La Torre, himself a Hispanic, speaks out in a voice from the margins and offers a different reading of this familiar story. What's actually happening, he says, is that God is asking Jonah — eight hundred or so years before the birth of Christ — to go to Nineveh, the center of the Assyrian Empire (now known as the modern city of Mosul in Iraq) and speak the truth to them about God's displeasure with their evil ways. Jonah recoils from this calling, as anybody in their right mind would and as most of us do when God asks us to do most anything that's a little terrifying. Instead, he heads for the coast, boards a ship, and does his best to disappear. He even tells a few of the members of the crew why he's taking this little cruise. So when the storm comes up, everyone figures it's Jonah's fault — after all, he's hiding out from God — and they throw him overboard, where he gets swallowed by a whale. And in the belly of that whale, Jonah tries to suck up to God: "You know best," he prays devoutly, "and we mortals don't." It's not recorded whether God was sickened by this attempt at flattery, but clearly the whale was, and he regurgitates Jonah up onto the beach.

At long last, Jonah makes his way to Nineveh, a nasty place populated by amazingly cruel people who made a habit of conquering smaller countries, killing off most of the population, and making the rest of them work for the empire. Assyria functioned the same way other empires did: it attacked and conquered marginalized communities, including the Hebrew people, and then used these conquered resources and people to sustain the empire.

So Jonah goes right into the middle of this brutal place and, in the Name of Jahweh, calls them to repentance. And much to his consternation and amazement, they repent. After all, one of the reasons Jonah didn't want to go to Nineveh in the first place was that he knew God to be merciful. And he was right. Sure enough, when the people repent, God cleans the slate and treats the Ninevites with kindness and mercy. But instead of rejoicing, Jonah is furious. He sulks and stalks off in a huff. And in so doing, contends De La Torre, he short-circuits the real work of reconciliation.

This is the surprising message of the Book of Jonah, as discerned by this "theologian from the margins." Jonah so hates his oppressors, the Ninevites, that he won't stick around long enough to finish the hard work of reconciliation that began only when he showed up in Nineveh with his message from God. Had Jonah stayed, he might have been able to teach the Assyrians about the ways of God and about the results of their destructive oppression of its conquered neighbors. Only then would real transformation of the empire have been possible. As it was, the people of Nineveh did what power and empire always do: they changed as little as they could get by with and still silence the conflict at hand, while mostly continuing their destructive and oppressive ways. They learned nothing about justice from the confrontation.

So what does the hard and holy work of reconciliation look like? If reconciliation comes from the margins and begins with the oppressed, what do the oppressed need to do?

First of all, suggests De La Torre, the oppressed need to forgive God for letting all this happen in the first place. The Hebrew scriptures, including the beloved Psalms, are full of people ranting and raving at God, expressing their anger and disappointment that oppression, pain, and suffering have befallen them, and then calling on God to do something to remedy the situation. The Hebrew scriptures clearly show a God who can withstand the anger of God's people. That's the first bit of grieving and letting go that the oppressed need to take care of.

Of course the responsibility for reconciliation doesn't begin and end with the oppressed, but for someone in an oppressed situation, freedom and liberation can come only after expressing and then letting go of anger. After all, maturity is reconciling yourself to the fact that you will never have a better past. Letting go of it makes reconciliation possible.

But then, for their *own* good, the oppressed need to forgive their oppressors. Note the emphasis here. This is not forgiveness for the good of the oppressors, to relieve them of their responsibility for their actions. This is forgiveness that serves to liberate the oppressed from the anger, fear, and hatred that only consumes them. Jonah, in holding on to his righteous anger, is held back from doing the work that would have brought his people — *and* his oppressors — true liberation and reconciliation.

The third thing the oppressed need to do is to recognize and embrace the fact that God wants the salvation of the oppressor. We have the same problem today that Jonah did. Jonah knew that God was merciful, and he hated that about God. He hated like crazy that God was willing to forgive the terrible Ninevites. He would have much preferred that God rain down fire upon his enemies, and he was disappointed that God was merciful instead, longing for their salvation as much as the salvation of the Jews. The fact is, regardless of our righteous indignation about it, God will simply be who God is, so we might as well get used to it.

Jesus is a perfect model of this. At the very moment of his crucifixion he prays for his tormentors, never losing the desire for his oppressors' salvation.

Ultimately, of course, the work of reconciliation can be complete only if the oppressors are somehow brought to see their own actions for what they are, and to understand that their oppression exacts a price from their own humanity, as well as from the oppressed. In the end, the oppressors must see that *they* are being diminished by the inhuman treatment of other human beings. Human nature and human sin being what it is, this last step of transformation can never be assured. Sometimes the evil has so infused the oppressors, and the self-interest served by the oppression seems so apparent, that the oppressors make no move at all toward transformation and reconciliation.

Instead, empire will most likely do everything it can to appease the current problem — as the Assyrian Empire did with Jonah and the Roman Empire did with Jesus — without making any substantive change. As De La Torre puts it,

> All too often reconciliation is reduced to negotiation, a bargaining process with the goal of reducing hostility, but with minimal change. Most often the goal of such an undertaking is not to bring forth justice and liberation, but to manage the disenfranchised, so that they better accept the prevailing social order.[2]

---

2. De La Torre, *Liberating Jonah*, 90.

There are lots of examples from our own time. Think, for instance, about politically correct language. I favor language that takes into account the sensitivities of people and issues, but politically correct language may have become our way of signaling that we've changed, when in fact we really have not. We all know, for example, how not to sound racist. But does anyone think for a minute that racism has gone away? We know how not to sound sexist, but has sexism diminished as much as our language indicates? We may have seduced ourselves into believing that our change of language reflects an equally genuine change of heart, but I'm not so sure that's the case.

Another example: I'm absolutely committed to the Millennium Development Goals, but God help us if in sending our money to worthy projects we congratulate ourselves on changing the system of empire that created unspeakable situations in the first place. If we wanted to get serious about real change, what would we do? We might start a boycott of Wal-Mart, which is telling their overseas suppliers exactly what they'll pay for a pair of shoes, regardless of the conditions they're manufactured under and who gets abused in the process. That kind of systemic change is what a commitment to the MDG's ought to signal. But just sending money isn't the change that's needed. The MDG effort shouldn't be an exercise in how little we can get away with doing, so that everybody (the poor, for instance) will calm down and things can stay the same.

Another example of this is the so-called "listening process" in the Anglican Communion. For twenty years — in 1978, 1988, and again in 1998 — the bishops of the Anglican Communion gathered at their once-a-decade Lambeth Conference and declared the need for the church to listen to the stories of its gay and lesbian members. Yet when the conference convenes again in 2008, little real listening will have gone on. Window dressing, posing as listening, is the order of the day. There seems to be little interest or desire for such listening to take place, and little courage by the church's leaders for leading the way. Many in the Communion are saying, "Let the listening process do its work, and then we'll get somewhere," while at the same time resisting any efforts to listen or to engage in dialogue. Empire, remember, will do what it can to *appear* to be open to transformation, without actually transforming.

Another example is our treatment of one another across racial divides. Blessed Desmond Tutu has wisely asked, "If you've taken my pen, then what good is your apology for taking my pen if you still have my pen?" The topic of reparations for the evils and enduring effects of slavery is a topic white people in this country simply refuse to discuss. "I'm not responsible for what happened years ago" is the standard retort of the white majority, meant to absolve those who still benefit from those evils at the expense of the descendants of slaves.

Reparations aside, many among the white majority like to denigrate and resist the notion of affirmative action. As white people, often quoting notions of equality in the Constitution, we in effect say we're sorry for being racist, and now that we have said we're sorry, let's have a level playing field. Let's treat everybody the same. But the fact is, the playing field is not equal *because* of centuries of oppression. The level playing field can begin only when that field is equal. Affirmative action is one strategy for getting there.

Reconciliation happens when someone comes from the margins and speaks the truth to power, and with great difficulty and turmoil, empire then rethinks its own history to include those who are marginalized — and then does something to set right the wrong in response.

Such a process is so difficult that it seems miraculous when it occurs. But most of us have been graced to witness it in our lifetimes. South Africa stands out as showing us the way forward — not a perfect example, of course, but a compelling one.

Reconciliation isn't just turning the tables and letting the oppressed become the oppressors. Had that happened, there would have been a bloodbath in South Africa. To be in South Africa today, one wonders how it *didn't* happen that way. But Nelson Mandela and Desmond Tutu had a different, holy vision and somehow communicated that vision to an entire oppressed majority.

It may feel good to do to them what they did to you, but it's not reconciliation, they preached. Reconciliation is incredibly costly for the oppressor because the reconciliation is achieved only when the oppressor makes amends. It's not just leveling the playing field and starting anew without taking responsibility for the way things have been in the past. But reconciliation is costly for the oppressed too, because it calls them to courageous action in telling the truth about the oppression they've endured.

Reconciliation, it seems, always involves convening a commission of one sort or another, and South Africa gave us a model for it. It involves courageously admitting what has been true and how it has been oppressive. It involves reliving painful memories of unspeakable violence and degradation for the oppressed; it involves an equally painful admission of the truth by the oppressors. The victimizer's admission of responsibility is crucial to the healing. It's important that the person who has perpetrated an injustice admit to the injustice. And even though the injustice can't be undone — you can't, after all, un-rape somebody — an acknowledgement of the awful truth is enormously helpful to the healing process for the person who has experienced the injustice. (De La Torre asks when we in America will have our own "truth and reconciliation commission" telling of the truth about our European-American ancestors' treatment of the indigenous peoples of this land and stop celebrating Columbus Day!)

The only hope for real reconciliation is taking seriously what Jesus said about loving our enemies. That's where Jonah got it

wrong. Jonah so hated the Ninevites and so begrudged their repentance that he didn't stick around to do the hard work of
reconciliation, which seeks nothing less than changing the world.

So what does all this teach me? I don't know what it teaches
those who are victims of racial injustice or gender injustice. But I
know what it teaches me from the perspective of being a gay man.

I was speaking at Colby College in Maine about how blessed
I feel to have experienced injustice because of being gay, because
it's made me understand a tiny bit of what it must be like to be
part of other oppressed groups. I much too flippantly added, "I
don't know how you straight, white males ever get it!" Afterward,
a young student came up to me and said, "I have an answer for
your question about how we straight white males 'get it.' I listen
to you, and then I believe you. I listen to what your truth is. It's
not a truth I know, but I believe it is your truth." Such wisdom
from a nineteen-year-old!

That's where we are at this moment in the Anglican Communion, and in the world at large. There are so many oppressions
going on, and almost everyone reading this book, in all likeli-
hood, is on the oppressor side of most of them. I know I am.
I'm white, I'm male, I'm American, I'm from the Global North,
I'm reasonably able-bodied, I'm educated. So it's only through
the experience of being gay, of being on the receiving end of oppression, that I've come to see the ways in which I am usually the
oppressor. The fact of the matter is that the only way for both
the oppressed and the oppressor to be free is to stay connected,
even committed, to one another.

The reason I am desperate to stay connected to the Global
South and to the Anglican Communion worldwide is that I need
them for my salvation. I don't know how else I'm going to learn
what it's like to be someone in the world subjected to my oppression and the oppression by communities of which I am a part—
males, Caucasians, Americans. How will I hear and learn about
the effects of the power and the hegemony of America if not for

the honest confrontation by people who have been its victims, whether in colonial days past or today?

Ian Douglas, professor of missiology at the Episcopal Divinity School, tells a story about a meeting he attended in Jamaica of a group within the Anglican Communion; most of the provinces of the Communion were represented. Someone remarked, "You have to understand that we don't see a lot of difference between George Bush and Gene Robinson. You must understand that what the American church has done in the election and consecration of Gene Robinson is in our eyes just another example of what America is doing around the world: having its own way, and the rest of the world be damned." As a white male American, will I ever really understand the injustice that I have participated in and still benefit from at the expense of others? Not unless someone from a marginalized group loves me enough to tell me what I don't want to hear. I need people of color to love me enough to tell me about their oppression at the hands of white people. I need women to point out my continuing benefit to being male in this society. And heterosexual people need their gay and lesbian brothers and sisters to tell them how their treatment of us diminishes us all. The possibility of our salvation and our transformation depends on it. That's why we need to hold together as the Episcopal Church and as the Anglican Communion.

So walking away from the table seems to be the worst sin of all. That's what Jonah did, and it short-circuited the hard work of reconciliation that God wanted. For reconciliation in the Anglican Communion today, both sides need to say as positively and authentically as we can that we want to be related to one another. As painful as it sometimes is for all of us, no matter where we fall on the various sides of the debate, we must stay connected — liberals and conservatives, evangelicals and Anglo-Catholics, Global South and Global North. We must name walking away from the table as the sin it is. And we must make our peace with — perhaps even embrace — the inevitable conflict that staying together will precipitate.

The ministry of reconciliation by its very nature involves conflict. It doesn't abolish conflict. When you love people enough to tell them a truth they don't want to hear, it gets pretty scary, and it stirs up anger and resistance. And when you start talking about the injustices that you've suffered at your oppressor's hands, it's never pretty. Just as there's no other way to Easter except through Good Friday, there's no other way to get to reconciliation. On the path to reconciliation, we'll hear things we don't want to hear, and the situation will probably get worse before it gets better. There are difficult truths that need to be spoken, but as scripture reminds us time and time again, we don't have to be afraid. Because the God who has seen us through the ages and wants very desperately for us the kind of reconciliation that ushers in real transformation will be there for us and with us every step of the way.

When Jesus said he came to bring a sword, not peace, I think he was talking about times like ours. It has to get pretty un-peaceful before we can get to real reconciliation. Maybe we won't live to see that reconciliation happen, but that's okay. One of my favorite places is the National Civil Rights Museum in Memphis, Tennessee. It's at the old Lorraine Motel, where Dr. Martin Luther King Jr. was assassinated. Because of racial segregation in the South, it was the only place that Dr. King could stay when he was in Memphis. In the lobby of the old hotel there's an enormous black granite monolith, and carved on it, in bas relief, is an ever-upwardly spiraling trail of African Americans. Up and up, and up and up, march these African Americans, every single one of them standing on someone else's shoulders. It's not necessary for us to live to see the finished product of reconciliation; it's enough for us to be a part of the march.

In the end, the only "expert" on reconciliation is Our Lord and Savior Jesus Christ. In his death on the cross, he has opened for us not only the gates of eternal life after death, but also the possibility of life before death. In refusing to demonize and hate his enemies, forgiving them and loving them to the very end, Jesus shows us the way to reconciliation. If we keep our eyes set on him, and upon his self-giving, self-sacrificing love, then we will know the way forward. Whatever difficulty may come, no matter how hard it gets, we will know how it eventually will end. We need not be afraid. God's fatherly saving grace will not be foiled, God's Son's sacrifice on the cross will not be in vain, and God's Holy Spirit will continue to lead us into reconciliation.

✳ 21 ✳

GOD IN THE DETAILS

God, working in the mysterious ways for which God is so widely renowned, seems to be working overtime in the Episcopal Church. Sometimes, in the heat of the moment, it doesn't seem like it, but I believe with all my heart that the Holy Spirit has worked through — of all things — the legislative processes of our every-three-years General Convention.

That's not to say I've been thrilled with everything that happened last time around, in 2006. But it's really important for us to continue to believe that as disappointing as outcomes sometimes are, the Holy Spirit works through the General Convention — even when we don't get our way, even if the church has a failure of nerve. All of us need to take heart. After all, we're in this for the long haul, and we can expect an assortment of bumps along the way. But nobody, ever, in the history of the universe, has made any progress in anything important — never mind anything to do with the rights and dignity of any group of people — that's proceeded in a straight line. We've always moved forward, and then moved back, and then moved forward and back again. So we must not lose hope, even, or maybe especially, in the bureaucracy of the Episcopal Church and the Anglican Communion. And, as with any family — just think back to last Christmas at your house — there's bound to be some fighting along the way.

Our Anglican difficulties today aren't really new. They're just a new chapter in a very old conflict that started a couple of thousand years ago, and the Holy Spirit has been there in the midst of every battle, large and small. People often ask me when this infighting will end. My response is always a rather pessimistic "never." Because just as soon as we make some serious progress on the gay and lesbian issue, God will point out somebody else we've been overlooking, just as God pointed out that we'd been excluding women and people of color and those who are differently abled. Remember that a lot of people said we didn't need to build handicapped access ramps because we didn't have anybody in wheelchairs. But when we built the ramps, we had disabled people coming out of the woodwork. God won't be finished with us until we do what God wants, which is to embrace all of God's children. It's just that simple.

We took a big step toward that embrace when we committed ourselves, at every level of the church, to the United Nations Millennium Development Goals. By working to eradicate extreme poverty and responding to diseases like malaria and AIDS, by seeking the empowerment of women and fostering education for children, we are putting the Gospel into action and welcoming the poorest of the poor into the loving embrace of Christ and his church.

If we live into that commitment, the African and Asian conservatives and the Anglican Communion at large will see that we are in communion with them. They'll understand that when we talk about inclusiveness, we mean business. And that will speak far louder than any covenant we ever signed, or any statement we've ever made. Signing on to the MDGs was really the most important thing we did at General Convention 2006, and we simply cannot let that get lost in all this other stuff. The debate around homosexuality in the church, much as Barbara Boxer, the Senator from California, said about the gay marriage debate, is a weapon of mass distraction. I am here to tell you what the homosexual agenda is: it is Jesus.

I believe that with my whole heart. And if you and I learn to talk about the God we know in our lives, who has transformed us, who has liberated us, who helps us believe that nothing can separate us from the love of God in Christ Jesus, if we learn to talk about that God in our lives, sooner or later our critics are going to see that the God we're talking about is the same God they know. And then the Communion will take care of itself. That's the witness that you and I have to make. After all, the Anglican Communion isn't just a vast bureaucracy. It's really the people, you and I, who make it up.

The Holy Spirit also led us during the General Convention into some territory I didn't much like. But as Christians we have to believe — in that back-and-forth way — that things are working together for good. Consider for example the issue of the Windsor Report and the issue of a moratorium on the election and consecration of bishops who happen to be gay. The one good thing about all this is that everybody was looking for a way forward, really. Everybody wanted to demonstrate as powerfully as we could that we mean to be a part of this wonderful, beloved Anglican Communion — as well as be true to who we are as a church and where God seems to be leading us in our context. And everybody's trying to find a way forward through that conundrum.

It wasn't the way that most gay and lesbian people in the church wanted, but the resolution passed. It wasn't so much a move forward, or even backward, but a way of hitting the pause button. One lay deputy — a former diocesan chancellor, tough as nails, brilliant, and openly lesbian — stood at the microphone and said: "You all know what a toll this will take on me, but I'm going vote yes." And because all of us wanted to support the new presiding bishop, and so wanted to give her everything she needed to have as she went off to her first primate's meeting, many voted yes. And almost immediately, the conservatives declared these sacrificial efforts to be grossly insufficient and began asking for alternative primatial oversight, and sowing the seeds of a split, about as cruel and awful a thing as I had seen Christians do to one another in a long time — all carefully orchestrated and strategized.

Will there be a split? I don't know. But I know that we have to hold our beloved presiding bishop's feet to the fire, so that she makes good on her pledge for the full inclusion of gay and lesbian people in the life of this church. And we'll find out if the rest of the Anglican Communion is committed to a conversation with us. We need to engage in those conversations and see if the rest of the Communion really wants to talk to us and wants to listen to our stories, and let us demonstrate that we want to listen to their stories.

As Christians, we know, from the scriptures and from our own experience, that the Holy Spirit is at work in moments big and small. On the Sunday afternoon of General Convention 2006, the Holy Spirit shifted into overdrive. All the bishops of the Episcopal Church gathered in Holy Trinity Church in Columbus, Ohio, and the doors were locked until we elected a new presiding bishop. When the candidates were named, months before, Katharine Jefferts Schori was clearly thought to be a fine nominee. But she was quite unknown in the House of Bishops, and she wasn't expected to win. People were just delighted that a woman had been named as a candidate. After a "meet the candidates" evening at a House of Bishops meeting, I heard people say, again and again, that they had never seriously considered Katharine, *but wasn't she something?* And on the day of the election, there were no campaigns for any of the candidates; there was no big strategy afoot, at least that I could detect, to elect any particular bishop.

Even though nobody thought Katharine had a prayer of being elected, many said they'd vote for her on the first ballot just as a way of saying, "You go, girl! Thank you for being in this mix and for being such a wonderful human being and bishop."

But when the results of the first ballot came back, Katharine was leading with about half the votes she needed. By the second ballot, when all these "courtesy" votes were expected to melt away, she'd added another five or six votes. With the third ballot, she'd picked up another fifteen votes, and she led for the whole rest of the way.

Coincidentally (or perhaps not!), around the walls of that church where we were gathered was a timeline of the role of women in the Episcopal Church in America. It went back as far as Virginia Dare, the first child baptized into the church in the 1600s, and continued up through the years, past brave women who claimed the ministry they had been given at their baptisms, through the Philadelphia 11, who had forced the issue of women's ordination, right through to Barbara Harris, the first woman bishop. And in that space we did this remarkable thing: we elected the church's first female presiding bishop. One of the men rushed over to the women's time line with a felt-tip pen to write in the latest installment of that movement of the Holy Spirit. It was extraordinarily moving. No one could believe what we had just done. It had been just thirty years from the time we voted for the ordination of women to the election of a woman as presiding bishop.

So back to the beginning. The Holy Spirit has been with us since the mighty winds of Pentecost, and we must continue to believe that the Holy Spirit is at work in this. We must not allow ourselves to see the Holy Spirit's action only when we get our way or win a vote. Like the Holy Spirit, we must take the long view, seeing our current struggles and debates in a broader, deeper context. Often the forces of darkness — and more often than not, that means the forces of fear — thwart the efforts of the Holy Spirit. That does not mean that the Spirit of God retreats, gives up, or loses hope. And neither should we.

The 2006 General Convention was just the latest example of our attempt to be the church, at this time in history and in our context. Those attempts will always be imperfect, always an im-pure mixture of motives. Once again we did some good and courageous things, and once again we shied away from others.

In the end I believe that the Holy Spirit shows up in the formal deliberations of the church and its councils. To the degree that we open ourselves to that Spirit, we do God's work. When we are too frightened to do the right thing, we sometimes do the wrong thing. Through it all the Spirit of God does not abandon us, but rather keeps coming back to inspire us and to lead us into all truth.

∗ 22 ∗

FAMILY REUNION

Every ten years since 1868 all the bishops of the Anglican Communion — that now adds up to over eight hundred men and a few women from all over the world — gather in England to study, talk, and pray together. It's a time to hammer out problems, share concerns, challenge and comfort one another, and remind ourselves of all the things we have in common as Christians and as Anglicans. It's not unlike a big family reunion, and mostly it's a good experience.

You've probably been to family reunions too. What could be better? You get to see Granny and Gramps, chat with Auntie Meg, and talk football with Cousin Joe. But then what about Uncle Ralph, who always has a little too much to drink and tends to get obnoxious, and Aunt Betty, who makes the world's worst potato salad and makes you eat some anyway? What about the arguments about politics and religion that you always seem to get drawn into by those ne'er-do-well cousins in the reprobate branch of the family? But still, they're all family, and somehow you all belong together at the same table.

But imagine getting a call from the family matriarch suggesting that it might be better if you just came for dessert, but not for the meal itself. Or maybe it would be better if you didn't come at all, since some members of the family have threatened not to come if you're there. That would be worse than strange. It would probably make you feel second class. And I bet it would make you feel disinclined to go. After all, a family reunion is for all those who are members of the family, and they're all invited because they're irrevocably linked by blood, regardless of their current "standing" in the family.

In May 2007, representatives of the Archbishop of Canterbury asked me to consent to doing just such a thing. With the Lambeth Conference fast approaching, the archbishop was seeking some way for me to attend the conference without offending conservative bishops who see my consecration as anathema to the Communion. I really do believe that the archbishop was trying to find a way forward that would offend the least number of people. Would I consider coming for only part of the time, and in a "diminished status"?

So what exactly would this diminished status look like? I was told that it might mean going to the Lambeth Conference, but not being assigned to a daily Bible study group. It might mean attending worship services, but not vesting as a bishop along with all the other bishops. And, I inquired, if I wasn't there in my official status as a bishop, what would they call my "diminished status"? Observer? Would I merely be asked to observe and not contribute? Guest? A guest is someone who is not a member of the family. Visitor? No different than the many who will attend to watch the goings-on? Nobody seemed quite sure what to do with me, or what to call me, that would assuage the objections from other members of the family.

Of course it was a tough decision to make. I talked with our presiding bishop twice about it, and I took trusted friends and colleagues into my confidence and tapped into their wisdom. I spent many days in intense prayer and discernment.

My initial negative reactions led me to a rather tortured self-searching. Am I being self-centered in worrying about my status? Could I do a generous and gracious thing for the Communion by attending Lambeth in a diminished status? Was the Archbishop of Canterbury offering an act of generosity that might win some hearts and minds among those who believe my consecration as a bishop of the church to be wrongheaded and unholy? Would my attendance in a diminished capacity "save" the Communion, at least for a little while? Couldn't I take such a lesser status if it served the church?

In the end, though, I simply had to respond with a respectful "no." I could not, at least right now, accept any status other than that accorded to any duly elected, consented to, and consecrated bishop of the church. And these are the reasons why.

It's Not Just about Me. This debate is not just about me, and therefore, this is not my sole decision to make. It was the Episcopal Church in New Hampshire that elected me; it was the Episcopal Church, acting as deputies (laity and clergy) and bishops, who consented to that election at the General Convention in Minneapolis in 2003. It was the Episcopal Church, represented by the nearly fifty bishops present, that consecrated me. It is the diocesan and national leadership of the Episcopal Church that has paid a high price for these actions and for their continued support of me in the meantime. It is the Episcopal Church — evidenced most recently in the Fall 2007 actions of our House of Bishops — that has, wisely or unwisely, chosen to move forward at what seems to us like the leading of the Holy Spirit. My agreeing to accept a diminished status at Lambeth would undercut and undermine the very progress we have made, as a church, at some considerable cost. And therefore, it is not for me as an individual to decide to be less than the church has called me to be and consecrated me to be.

This Won't Go Away. I am often asked why I don't step down and just end this mess. The fact is, if I were hit by a bus and killed tomorrow, this would not go away. There are faithful, skilled, experienced, and otherwise qualified gay and lesbian members of this church who will be elected bishop in their dioceses. My diminished status at Lambeth — or my simply staying home — would not change that. Does anyone, liberal or conservative, really believe that this controversy will go away if I disappear?

Why Should I Fall on My Sword? If I am willing to be at the table with those who have called me "lower than the dogs" and "Satan entering the church," why are those conservatives — whom I have never publicly criticized, much less demonized — unwilling to be at the table with me? Why is it a greater risk for them than for me? And why aren't they being called to account for their actions and their words? While pastoral concern continues to be expressed in various communiqués for the church's gay and lesbian members, draconian measures to penalize and even imprison gay people are supported by Anglican leaders in some of the Communion's provinces, without a public word of criticism from the Archbishop of Canterbury. Is the Archbishop of Canterbury's concern for how many might join a boycott of Lambeth by Nigerian archbishop Peter Akinola so great that he refuses to hold them accountable for their un-Christian behavior? Does the archbishop really believe that my coming to Lambeth in a diminished status — or not at all — would alter their actions and words that harm gay and lesbian Christians everywhere? What evidence does he have that such would be the case?

Exclusion Won't Move Us Forward. Exclusion from Bible study, or from any group in which someone might be uncomfortable with my presence, deprives all of us of the opportunity to build community, through the common study of scripture and thoughtful conversation. How would my exclusion from such conversations model the listening process that has been proposed by every Lambeth Conference for the last thirty years? Would it not model the opposite? Is this the model for listening we really want to promote? Excluding me from participating as a bishop tries to deny the legitimacy of my consecration by the church. How can this possibly move us forward?

No Place at the Table. I would be able to attend Lambeth knowing that unspeakable things will be said to me and about me. I could fully participate, knowing that there is terrible animosity surrounding me from those who believe I should not be a bishop, or even ordained. But I'm not sure I can survive three weeks of "playing nice," accepting a non-place at the table, being tolerated at best, watching other bishops take their place in procession. It's not unlike a field slave, soon after the Emancipation Proclamation, being invited up to the Big House, but told he can still only be there as a slave, not as a guest at the host's table. That feels unconscionably demeaning. And frankly, gay and lesbian people have been demeaned, demonized, and rejected for far too long. I'm just not sure I could do it. As close as God seems, as faithfully present as God has been for me throughout all this, I'm not sure I could trust myself to trust God enough to help me survive a three-week daily assault on my integrity, my humanity, and my ministry.

◆ ◆ ◆

A few months after my consecration as bishop in 2003, I suggested to the Archbishop of Canterbury that, in light of the controversy within the Communion, I'd be willing to at least entertain the idea of attending Lambeth in a diminished status. He did not take me up on that offer. Back then, I thought I could do it. I thought it might help heal the wounds of my controversial election and bring all of us together as a family. But now I know different.

I have learned in dealing with congregations in conflict that the best way forward is to support and encourage the healthiest people and the healthiest groups within the congregation, encouraging their positive behavior in the face of destructive, adolescent bullying from other parts of the congregation. Why does the archbishop seem so paralyzed by the most extreme conservatives in our Communion? What is to be gained by giving in to the unreasonable demands of a few, or to tolerate their violation of diocesan and provincial boundaries? Bullies never get enough: they always come back for more and more, and in the end, unless their bluff is called, they will destroy every bit of health and integrity in the community. I would argue that the archbishop should invite *everyone* to Lambeth, and instead of making decisions based on what some *might* do, allow each bishop to choose whether or not to attend. This would take the responsibility off the archbishop, and put it squarely where it belongs — with each bishop of the Communion. The archbishop would be excluding no one, though some might choose to exclude themselves. This would be an honorable and defensible approach. If some chose not to show up, the Lambeth Conference would proceed with the people committed to the Communion and willing to work together, despite our differences.

This may be easy for me to suggest and hard for the archbishop to do, but I believe it is the best way forward. We need the archbishop to demand that we all be at the table and *stay* at the table, for our own good and for the good of the church. Anyone who refuses to participate in the Holy Eucharist and the study of the holy scriptures with any other Christian member of the Anglican family should be sent home. If we cannot read scripture and share the holy bread and wine of Communion with one another, the Communion is *already* lost.

✳ 23 ✳

FINDING HOME:
THE MIRACLE OF COMMUNION

I'm as far away from home as I've ever been. In the Solomon Islands, in the Anglican Province of Melanesia, staying with a diocesan bishop on this remote Pacific island.

The bishop's residence is hardly a palace; he lives in a sparely furnished, modest house, partly covered with a thatched roof. There is almost no food, but somehow, as if by magic, meals seem to appear — bread bought at a local bakery for breakfast; a handful of meat for supper, cooked into a stew with vegetables and poured over a huge bowl of rice. Each of us has a spoon — the only cutlery in the house.

Cold water is available for about two hours here and there during the day. Electricity is on again, off again. Hard-shelled bugs scamper across the floor. Rats the size of cats appear just outside the doorway. The only sign of twenty-first century life is a small laptop, hooked up to an agonizingly slow dial-up connection.

The bishop is host to a large household. It's not uncommon in this part of the world for young men — too old to remain at home, but not yet ready for marriage — to live in men's households, and nearly a dozen such young men live here. The bishop provides them with a social and moral compass in their formative years. I begin to understand just a bit of their pidgin language, which adds to the universal sign language we all use to communicate when words fail us. I am welcomed as a brother in Christ.

This hard-working missionary bishop has a tough row to hoe. Some of his parishes are nearby, of course, but some are a difficult journey away — perhaps a couple of days in a car, many hours in a canoe, and finally two or three days' walk into the bush. I feel very spoiled when I think of my complaints about a four-hour drive on good highways to my remotest parish, near the Canadian border.

It's hot here, near the equator. Most of life is lived outside. We sit around at night, talking. I'm fresh meat for the mosquitoes. It's hard not to think about the fact that everyone here has chronic malaria — and I may be next.

One of the local priests learns of the death of his uncle and asks if I'd like to accompany him back to his village to pay his respects. I am honored to be his companion. We must leave immediately because in this equatorial heat, the body cannot be held from burial for long. A tortuous jeep ride, dodging potholes and passing village after village, brings us to this priest's ancestral home. As we approach, we can hear the women wailing the loss of this important man in the community's life.

First off, we go to pay our respects to the chief, whose dwelling, standing up on stilts, is the only one that looks like a real house to Western eyes. Then we make our way to where the body lies. This is a large village, perhaps a thousand men, women, and children, all of them scantily clad. Clothes don't make much sense here, and I feel terribly overdressed. No one runs for shelter when an afternoon cloudburst opens up. After all, there are no clothes to change into, and besides, you dry off quickly in the equatorial heat.

The young girls are weaving magnificent wreaths for the burial: fragrant mangipany, colorful hibiscus, and exotic orchids, which grow at the edges of the village, all arranged in beautiful, symmetrical designs.

We walk over to the church. This priest's grandfather led his tribe down from the mountains and out of the bush when the Anglican missionaries settled here in the early 1900s. He is buried in the place of honor, just at the bottom of the steps leading into the church. Off to the side, between the church and the bay, lies this priest's father's grave, and beside it, a hole already dug for his brother, who lies in state.

Here by the church there's no electricity, and the water comes from a communal well. No possessions are in evidence besides the clothes people are wearing on their backs. I see no books, no furniture, no "stuff." I can't help but wonder what people do all day, what they talk about, what they hope for. My Western mind, tuned to accomplishing things in the American entrepreneurial tradition, wonders how these people fill the hours of every day, beyond providing for life's basic necessities. Although I surely don't feel that my life is better because of the things I own, I ponder what life would be like with so little. It would be easy to wax romantic about such a simple life on a sun-drenched Pacific island, but I'm not convinced that there's anything romantic about it. Still, a life stripped of things and distractions has a certain appeal.

Perhaps as many as five hundred people are sitting around the thatched hut on stilts that holds the body. Naked children are sitting in the laps of their parents or brothers and sisters. Everyone is quiet — either out of respect for the dead, or because they're curious about the white guy wearing a pectoral cross who's just arrived.

We remove our shoes and climb the little ladder that leads up to the house. There is no furniture inside. It is dark, even though it's the middle of the day. The women continue their wailing as family members sit with the body. The priest I'm with asks to see the body of his uncle. The women begin to uncover the man, beginning with the cloths that shroud his body. The final covering is a layer of banana leaves, which, when peeled back, reveal the man's face. A new wave of wailing possesses the women as the dead man's face appears. We silently attend the dead. And then the priest announces that "the bishop will now pray."

Surprisingly, the wailing stops. Immediately. It's then that I realize that while these women obviously knew the deceased and mourn his passing, they are performing a ritual, liturgical role as wailers. Their cries do not need to wind down gradually in an effort to control their grief because they are here to do a job. All goes silent.

I begin to pray: for the deceased, for the family, for the village. I give thanks for his father and his role in leading this tribe to this place, and ultimately, being responsible for their conversion, and their Anglican expression of that conversion. None of which anyone understands, except for the priest I'm with.

And then it happens. The miracle of communion. I begin to close the prayer and I decide to bless the people. It's what a bishop does. And as I say the words, "in the Name of the Father, and of the Son, and of the Holy Spirit," everyone in this tiny hut crosses themselves. And in that moment, I am home.

They probably hadn't understood a word I'd said before that, or after. But they did understand that this priest and nephew had brought a brother in Christ to pay respects to the dead. I had traveled seventeen thousand miles to be here. On the surface, these people and I shared almost nothing in common except our humanity. Their lives could not be more different from mine. I could no more imagine what it would be like to live their lives than they could imagine living mine.

And yet, in that mystical moment and at the uttering of those holy words that have blessed and cured and comforted Christians for twenty centuries, all the difference between us is erased into matters of no significance. And in that moment we are One, bound by our love of Jesus Christ and our experience of a loving God. Here is the Anglican Communion, on full display in a small hut perched high on stilts, beside a beautiful bay, in a group of islands somewhere in the vast Pacific. And at the invocation of "Father, Son, and Holy Spirit" we remember who we are and are reminded that we are One because of *whose* we are. And though I am halfway around the globe from where I live, I am home.

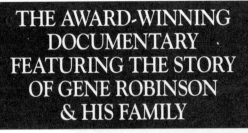
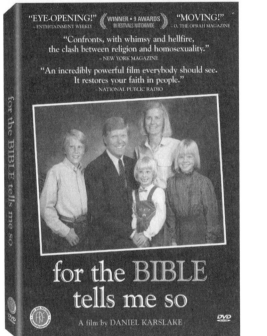